SECOND GRADE

TIMBERDOODLE'S CURRICULUM HANDBOOK

2019- 2020 EDITION

"TOWER" COVER ART BY CLARK NATHANIEL, AGE 7
"SQUIRREL" COVER ART BY AVA SCHOESSOW, AGE 10
ALL THE AMAZING INTERIOR DOODLES PROVIDED BY OUR TALENTED CUSTOMERS

Welcome to **Second Grade**

WE'RE SO GLAD YOU'RE HERE!

Congratulations on choosing to homeschool this year! Whether this is your first year as a teacher or your tenth, we're confident you'll find that there is very little that compares to watching your child's learning take off. In fact, teaching can be quite addictive, so be forewarned!

ON YOUR MARK, GET SET, GO!

Preparing for your first "school day" is very easy. Peruse this guide, look over the typical schedule, browse the introductions in your books, and you will be ready to go.

GET SUPPORT

Are you looking for a place to hang out online with like-minded homeschoolers? Do you wonder how someone else handled a particular science experiment? Or do you wish you could encourage someone who is just getting started this year? Join one or more of our Facebook groups.

Timberdoodlers of all ages:
https://www.facebook.com/groups/Timberdoodle/

Timberdoodlers with 1st- to 4th-grade students:
www.facebook.com/groups/ElementaryTimberdoodle

SCHEDULE CUSTOMIZER

Your 2019-2020 Second-Grade Curriculum Kit includes access to our Schedule Customizer, where you can not only adjust the school weeks, but also tweak the checklist to include exactly what you want on your schedule. To get started, just click the link in your access email and visit the scheduling website!
www.TimberdoodleSchedules.com

If you ordered through a charter school or don't have that link for some other reason, just email schedules@Timberdoodle.com and we'll get that sorted out ASAP. (Including your order number will really speed that process up for you.)

WE WILL HELP

We would love to assist you if questions come up, so please don't hesitate to contact us with any questions, comments, or concerns. Whether you contact us by phone, email, or live online chat, you will get a real person who is eager to serve you and your family.

YOU WILL LOVE THIS!

This year you and your student will learn more than you hoped while having a blast. Ready? Have an absolutely amazing year!

CONTENTS

ITEM-BASED RESOURCES

WHEN YOU'RE DONE HERE

MEET YOUR HANDBOOK

WELCOME TO YOUR TEACHING TOOLBOX!

Simple Is Better
We really believe that, so your guide is as simple as we could make it.

1. The Planning
First up are all the details on planning your year, including your annual planner and sample weekly checklists, the absolute backbones of Timberdoodle's curriculum kits. More on those in a moment.

2. Reading Challenge
Next up is the reading challenge, complete with book ideas to give you a head start.

3. Item-by-Item Details
We then include short bios of each item in your kit, ideal for refreshing your memory on why each is included, or to show off exactly what your second-grader will be covering this year. This is where we've tucked in our tips or tricks to make this year more awesome for all of you.

4. Teacher Resources
In this section you'll find our favorite articles and tidbits amassed in our more-than-30 years of homeschool experience.

5. Items with Special Instructions
Finally, we'll conclude with specific book ideas for your reading challenge this year, as well as 36 ideas for using Mad Mattr.

All the Details Included
This Timberdoodle curriculum kit is available in three different standard levels: Basic, Complete, or Elite. This allows you to choose the assortment best suited to your child's interest level, your family's schedule, and your budget. In this guide, you'll find an overview and any tips for each of the items included in the Elite Curriculum Kit. If you purchased a Basic or Complete kit, or if you customized your kit, you chose not to receive every item, so you'll only need to familiarize yourself with the ones which were included in your kit.

Don't Panic, You Didn't Order too Much Stuff!
We know you. OK, maybe not you personally, but we have yet to meet a homeschooler who doesn't have other irons in the fire. From homesteading or running a business to swimming lessons or doctor's appointments, your weeks are not dull. As you unpack your box you may be asking yourself how you'll ever fit it all in.

We'll go in-depth on schedules momentarily, but know now that most of the items in your kit feature short lessons, not all of them should be done every day, and your checklist is going to make this incredibly manageable. Really!

TIPS & TRICKS

YOUR FIRST WEEK, STATE LAWS, AND MORE

Week 1 Hints

As you get started this year, realize that you are just getting your sea legs. Expect your studies to take a little longer and be a little less smooth than they will be by the end of the year. As you get your feet under you, you will discover the rhythm that works best for you! If you don't know where to begin each day, why not try starting with something from the Thinking Skills category? It will get your child's brain in gear and set a great tone for the rest of the day.

Find Your Pace

We asked parents who used this kit how long their students spent on "school." Most said that they spent within 2-5 hours a day. That is not only a wide variation, but it also means some were outside that window. Make sure you allow yourself and your child some time to find your own rhythm!

Books First, or Not?

Some goal-oriented students might like to start each day with bookwork and end with fun, hands-on time. Others might prefer to intersperse the hands-on thinking games, STEM, and so forth between more intensive subjects to give their brains a clean slate.

A Little Every Day, or All at Once?

Depending on your preferences, your child's attention span, and what other time commitments you have (teaching other children, doctor appointments, working around a baby's nap), there are many different ways to schedule your week. Some families like to do a little portion from nearly all subjects every day, while others prefer to blast out an entire week's work within a subject in a single sitting. Throughout the year, you can tinker around with your daily scheduling and see what approach works best for your family.

Tips for Newbies

If you're new to homeschooling, it might be helpful for you to know that some subjects are typically taught and practiced several times a week for the best mastery. These would include basic math instruction, phonics, and spelling. However, more topical subjects such as geography, history, and science are often taught all at once. Meanwhile, thinking skills, STEM, and art, plus hands-on learning and games, can be even more tailored to the preferences of the child or used for independent learning while you are busy.

What About the Courses Which You Don't Work on Every Week?

As you go over your checklist, you'll notice that some of your courses are "2-3 a month" or "as desired," and that may leave you confused on how to tackle them. Here are a few other options: You could go ahead and do it every week, completing the course early. You could set aside the item for summer (see below). Or complete it as directed, of course!

The Summer Plan

If you're looking at all these tools and feeling a little overwhelmed, or if you just wish you had more structured activities for the summer, feel free to grab a handful of items from the kit and set them aside for summer. Then, set a reminder on your phone or calendar to remind you which ones they are and where you stashed them so you won't forget to use them!

Meeting State Requirements

Check https://www.hslda.org/laws to see the most current information on your specific requirements. For many states, it is sufficient to simply hang on to your completed and dated weekly checklists along with a sampling of your child's best work this year. Some states ask you to add in a state-specific topic or two, such as Vermont history, or a generic course like P.E. or Health. We have a summary on our blog comparing your kit to their requirements, but HSLDA is the gold standard for current legal information.

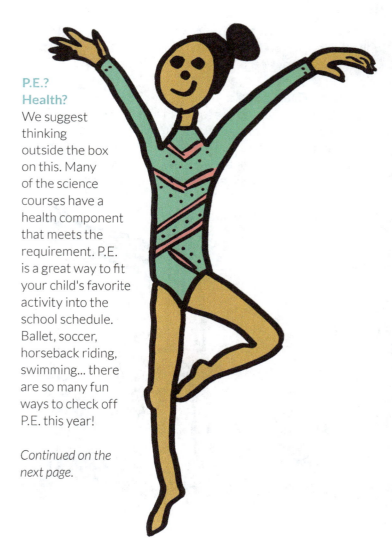

P.E.? Health?

We suggest thinking outside the box on this. Many of the science courses have a health component that meets the requirement. P.E. is a great way to fit your child's favorite activity into the school schedule. Ballet, soccer, horseback riding, swimming... there are so many fun ways to check off P.E. this year!

Continued on the next page.

TIPS & TRICKS, CONT.

Put Your Child in Charge?

The weekly checklists are the framework of your week, designed for maximum flexibility. Just check off each item as you get it done for the week and you'll be able to see at a glance that you still need to do __ this week. (This is true of the daily checklists as well - just on a shorter schedule.) Many students even prefer to get all their work done early in the week and enjoy all their leisure time at once!

Do Hard Things and Easy Ones

Our family provides foster care for kids who need a safe place for a while. This has exposed us to a whole new world of hard days and stressful weeks. If your child is struggling today, you are not failing if you take a step back and have him start with his most calming project. For our crew, often

that would be art or the reading challenge. You even have a little slush room in most subjects, so don't hesitate to trim the lessons short on a busy or challenging week, or pause schoolwork today for a complete reset and tackle it fresh tomorrow.

At the same time, you are not doing your child any favors if you never teach him how to work through a challenge. After all, you have hard days as a parent and still get up, drink your coffee, and jump back in. Be aware of your own tendency to have your child either buckle down and push through or to let him ease off completely, then work to provide a healthy balance for your child, particularly if he is in the process of healing.

Pro Tip

When you first get out a week's checklist, go ahead and check off all the things you don't need to do this week. For instance, if your child did a few extra pages of math last week or isn't ready for the readers, check those off. Doesn't that feel better?

The Sample Schedules

We're including a sample annual planner on page 16, followed by sample weekly planners for each level of your kit, reflecting a typical 36-week school year. This lets you see at a glance how this might work for you, even before you get a moment to sit down at your computer and print your own custom-fitted schedule.

ASK YOUR SECOND-GRADER!

A JUST-FOR-FUN BEGINNING OF THE YEAR INTERVIEW

Jot down your child's answers here to capture a fun time capsule of his second-grade year.

1. If you were to invent a game, what kind of game would that be? (board game, card game, outdoor activity...)

2. What is your favorite joke?

3. What is your favorite story or book?

4. What kind of things would you like to build? (tents, blocks, forts, crafts...)

5. What is your favorite winter activity? (Is there more than one?)

6. What is your favorite summer activity? (Is there more than one?)

7. What is something you look forward to doing when you grow up? (drive a car, do a special sport...)

8. Where is your favorite place?

9. What's your favorite food? (How do you make it?)

10. What do you want to be when you grow up?

MEET YOUR ONLINE SCHEDULER

GETTING THE MOST OUT OF YOUR PLANNERS

Use the Customizer

On the next pages you'll find sample weekly checklists for Basic, Complete, and Elite kits. Before you photocopy 36 of them, though, take a moment to check out the custom online schedule builder that came free with your kit. You'll not only easily adjust the weeks, but also tweak the checklist to include exactly what you want listed. Plus, you'll be able to print your weekly checklists directly from the schedule builder so you don't have to do that by photocopying! www.TimberdoodleSchedules.com

Activating Your Account

Before you can get started, you'll need your account activated for the online schedule builder. If you didn't get an activation email (perhaps you ordered through a charter school so we didn't have your email address), shoot us a quick email at schedules@Timberdoodle.com and we'll get that straightened out ASAP. Including your order number really speeds that process up, but our team is skilled at finding your activation info with whatever order data you have.

What's Your Dream Schedule?

Now that you're ready you'll want to know two things:

1. How Many Weeks Do You Want to Do School?

A standard school year is 36 weeks + breaks. Some families prefer to expedite and complete the entire year in fewer weeks - a great option for those of you who'd like to get all this year's school done before baby arrives, for instance. Or perhaps your family, like ours, prefers to school year-round and keep that brain sharp.

2. What Breaks Do You Want?

(Thanksgiving, Christmas, winter break, spring break... you could also add in weeks off that you're traveling, have guests, baby is coming, or...)

Typically you'll be adding full-week breaks only, so unless you're traveling to Disneyland® for little Owen's birthday, you don't need to add that to the calendar. For single-day breaks you'll likely prefer to just shuffle the work to earlier/later in the same week and keep on task otherwise. If you're using a daily schedule (see next page), though, you may find it worth your time to enter days off as well.

Choosing Your Items

Now just pop that data into the online schedule and scroll down to see the items you might have in your kit. Unchecking the boxes for any items you don't have removes them from your list. You'll also see "Alternative Items" listed under each subject. This usually includes all of our most popular customizations for this grade so that you can simply check a box and switch the scheduler to third-grade math, for instance.

Add Custom Courses

Your course list is limited only by your imagination. Perhaps your friend wrote you a custom curriculum you'd like to include, your family makes up a band and you'd like to have practice on this list, or you need to list ballet since that's P.E.

this year. At the very bottom of the page you'll find a place to add in just as many courses as you'd like. Just walk through the prompts on-screen to get it all set up.

Tweak It to Perfection

Do you have everything set? On the next screen you'll have some fun options.

Continued on the next page.

MEET YOUR ONLINE SCHEDULER, CONT.

1. Large Font Edition
Want a large-font option? Just check the box. If you don't like how it looks you can always come back and uncheck it.

2. Show Dates
Check this box if it's helpful for you to see at a glance that week 17 is January 13th-17th, for instance. Some teachers find this incredibly helpful while others prefer to move breaks around on the fly, making the dates irrelevant.

3. Weekly or Daily?
We prefer a weekly schedule, for the simple reason that our weeks are rarely without some anomaly. Off to the dentist's Tuesday? You won't fall behind by taking a day off.

Or perhaps you have Friday Robotics Camp for a couple of weeks and need to get all the week's work done over four days instead of five. No problem! This approach also teaches time-management skills (see the article on Independent Learning at the back of this book).

However, we've heard from many of you that having a daily schedule, especially for the first month, is a real life saver. So we developed one, and if it helps you, fantastic! The daily scheduler is programmed to split up the work as evenly as possible over the week, with the beginning of the week having any extra pages or lessons. (We all know that end-of-the-week doldrums are a real thing!)

Moving Courses to Certain Days
If you're opting for the daily scheduler, you do have some helpful fine-tuning options. Just click "Edit" on the course

in question and you'll have the option of selecting on which days of the week the course will appear. This lets you do things like schedule history only on Wednesday because that is co-op day. Or, you could schedule science only on Tuesday or Thursday and STEM on Friday or Monday so that science and STEM are never on the same day.

Pro Tip
You can also opt to exclude an item from certain weeks. This is useful if you already know that you want to save an art kit for May so that Grandma can do it with Owen or if you don't want to break out the graphic novel until after Christmas since you've set it aside as a gift.

4. Show Unit Range?
This feature sounds so very data-y and not super helpful, but we think you just might love it. Instead of saying that you

need to do seven pages of math this week, check this box to have it remind you that you're on worksheets 50-56 this week, for example. If you prefer extreme flexibility, leave this box unchecked. But if you're afraid of falling behind without knowing it, this box will be your hero.

Make More Lists

If you have one student and one teacher, you may feel free to buzz past this idea. But if you have an extra teacher– perhaps your spouse, a grandparent, or even an older sibling who wants the bonding time, then this may simplify your life! Instead of putting all of your child's work on a single list, you could put all the subjects you will teach on your list and all of the remaining subjects on "Grandma's list" for her ease.

If you have twins or multiple students at the same grade level, you can also make multiple lists to best meet each student's needs.

That's It!

Click Generate Schedule, then View Generated Schedule and you're ready to print it and get started!

FYI, our scheduler is constantly being improved, so for the most current instructions please refer to the blog link in your activation email.

Ideas Our Team is Working On

At the time of this printing, our team is working to add a time log to these lists for those of you whose states require it. We're also adding a way to easily email the schedule to yourself for your records, adding a progress report, and

fine-tuning how you add time off to your schedule. These are all features that you may expect to see more about on the above-mentioned blog post. Also, please let us know if you think of more features that our team should consider!

	CURRICULUM	LESSONS OR PAGES	= PER WEEK
Language Arts	All About Reading Level 3	54 lessons	20 minutes a day
	Daily 6-Trait Writing	25 weeks	1 week's work
	Spelling You See C	36 weeks	1 week's work
	My First Story Writing Book	30 activities	1 activity
	Lost Trail	64 pages	1-2 pages
	Word Fun	8 chapters	1 a month
Math	Math-U-See Beta	30 lessons	1 lesson, 7 worksheets
	Tenzi and Card Deck	unlimited	1 game
Thinking Skills	Building Thinking Skills 1	327 pages	9 pages
	Squirrels Go Nuts Logic Game	60 challenges	1-2 challenges
	Q-bitz Solo	40 challenges	2 challenges
History & Social Studies	The Story of the World 2	42 chapters	1-2 chapters
	Skill Sharpeners Geography	132 pages	3-4 pages
	This Is the World	16 destinations	1 destination
	Famous Figures of the Renaissance	10 figures	1-2 a month
Science	Science in the Ancient World	90 lessons	2-3 lessons
STEM	Engino Inventor 50	50 models	1-2 models
	Pixio 200	unlimited	2+ models
	Wile E. Coyote	104 pages	2-3 pages
Art	Me: A Compendium	98 pages	2-3 pages
	Natural World Workshop	4 projects	as desired
	Step-by-Step Drawing Book	47 projects	1-2 projects
	Fish Rainbows	4 pictures	as desired
Etc.	Mad Mattr	unlimited	as desired
	Spectrum Test Practice	154 pages	end of school year

YOUR ANNUAL PLANNER

WHAT IS A LESSON?

ITEM BY ITEM SPECS

On pages 32-64 you'll find an overview of each item, including information about how we split up the work and why, but if you're looking for a quick reference page to refresh your mind on what exactly "one lesson" means for any of your materials, here you go!

All About Reading Level 3
Time based - just do 20 minutes a day.

Daily 6-Trait Writing
Split into 25 weeks of work. We suggest starting this after 11 weeks of school to make sure your student is ready.

Spelling You See C
There are 36 lessons, each of which includes five days of work. Two tips: your day's lesson is complete after 10 minutes of work - your child does not need to finish that chunk. Also, if you're using a four-day week or otherwise don't get to all five days of work in a week, it is expected that you will still count that lesson as complete at the end of the week and move to the next one.

My First Story Writing Book
Each activity is spread over two pages and ranges from "fill in a diary page for any of these characters" to finishing off the endings for a variety of phrases. Do one spread a week.

Lost Trail
Hand this to your child for free reading, or assign 10 minutes twice a week, or two pages a week.

Word Fun
Covers eight parts of speech. Either complete one part of speech each month to get through the book once, or read one part of speech every week to get through it four times this year. Unless these are all terms that your child is comfortable using (nouns, adjectives, etc.), we suggest the faster pace to cement the concepts.

Math-U-See
You'll find 30 lessons here, each with seven worksheets. Since you'll only be completing as many of the worksheets as your child needs per lesson, and since completing one whole lesson a week keeps the instructional portions predictable, we suggest doing one lesson a week instead of a certain number of worksheets. If you use that method, know that you can spread a tricky lesson over two weeks up to six times this year without messing up your schedule.

Tenzi Game
Unlimited. We suggest pulling it out at least once a week.

Building Thinking Skills 1

There are 327 pages in this delightful (and substantial!) book. You'll want to do nine a week to stay on task for completion this year. Or, split it over two years, and do four to five pages a week.

Squirrels Go Nuts

Just do one to two new challenges a week, adding in as many "old" ones as your child would like.

Q-bitz Solo

Add two cards a week, following the progression of difficulty on page 49 in this handbook.

The Story of the World 2

With 42 chapters, you're going to want to do 3 chapters every two weeks. Or, if it's easier, just do 2 chapters one week and 1 chapter the following week. Add in as many activities as you have the time/interest for.

Skill Sharpeners Geography

While you could divide this by page numbers, we think you'll prefer to split it by activity pages. So you'll want to complete any instructional pages needed as well as about two activities a week.

This Is the World

With 16 destinations, we suggest reading about 1 a week, as that will take you through the entire book twice this year.

Famous Figures of the Renaissance

There are 10 models to complete here, each with a full-color and a color-it-yourself option. See page 51 for where those figures appear in Story of the World or just add one to your studies each month.

Science in the Ancient World

You'll see that some of the lessons in this book are color-coded red. These are optional lessons, so if you're trying to streamline your days, feel free to skip those and only do two lessons a week. If you want to do all the lessons, plan on three a week.

Continued on the next page.

Engino Inventor

Between the booklet and the online plans, there are 50 models to complete. Simply do 1-2 a week.

Pixio 200

Unlimited. We suggest completing at least two models a week - one from the app and one that's their own design.

Wile E. Coyote

There are 104 pages in all, so simply reading 2-3 a week will get you through all the books.

Me: A Compendium

Contains 51 spreads, including the cover/over-wrap, so your child will do 1-2 spreads a week.

Natural World Workshop

With four lovely paintings to complete, we suggest working on one a month, ideally spending about 20 minutes a week on it.

Step-by-Step Drawing Book

Includes 47 projects, (How to Draw a City, How to Draw a Tiger...), each ranging from one to two pages. Just do one or two drawing projects per week.

Fish Rainbows

There are another four stunning sand-art canvases to complete in this kit. Like Natural World Workshop we suggest working on one a month, ideally spending about 20 minutes a week on it.

Mad Mattr

Unlimited. We suggest pulling it out at least once a week, or whenever your child needs a fidget.

Spectrum Test Practice

We usually save this for the end of the year to refresh the student on all the skills he'll need for annual testing. You won't find this on your schedule unless you add it.

Language Arts	All About Reading Level 3	20 mins a day									
	Daily 6-Trait Writing	1 week's work									
	Spelling You See C	1 week's work									
Math	Math-U-See Beta	a 7-worksheet lesson									
Thinking Skills	Building Thinking Skills 1	9 pages									

Subject	Item	Amount							
Language Arts	All About Reading Level 3	20 mins a day							
	Daily 6-Trait Writing	1 week's work							
	Spelling You See C	1 week's work							
	My First Story Writing Book	1 activity							
Math	Math-U-See Beta	a 7-worksheet lesson							
	Tenzi and Card Deck	1 game							
Thinking Skills	Building Thinking Skills 1	9 pages							
	Squirrels Go Nuts Logic Game	1-2 challenges							
History & Social Studies	The Story of the World 2	1-2 chapters							
	Skill Sharpeners Geography	3-4 pages							
Science	Science in the Ancient World	2-3 lessons							
STEM	Engino Inventor 50	1-2 models							
Art	Me: A Compendium	2-3 pages							
	Natural World Workshop	as desired							
	Step-by-Step Drawing Book	1-2 projects							

Language Arts	All About Reading Level 3	20 mins a day						
	Daily 6-Trait Writing	1 week's work						
	Spelling You See C	1 week's work						
	My First Story Writing Book	1 activity						
	Lost Trail	1-2 pages						
	Word Fun	1 a month						
Math	Math-U-See Beta	a 7-worksheet lesson						
	Tenzi and Card Deck	1 game						
Thinking Skills	Building Thinking Skills 1	9 pages						
	Squirrels Go Nuts Logic Game	1-2 challenges		CIRCIT MAZE				
	Q-bitz Solo	2 challenges						
History & Social Studies	The Story of the World 2	1-2 chapters						
	Skill Sharpeners Geography	3-4 pages						
	This Is the World	1 destination						
	Famous Figures of the Renaissance	1-2 a month						
Science	Science in the Ancient World	2-3 lessons						
STEM	Engino Inventor 50	1-2 models		GRAVI TRAX				
	Pixio 200	2+ models						
	Wile E. Coyote	2-3 pages						
Art	Me: A Compendium	2-3 pages						
	Natural World Workshop	as desired						
	Step-by-Step Drawing Book	1-2 projects						
	Fish Rainbows	as desired						

THE READING CHALLENGE

BASED ON THE READING CHALLENGE FOR KIDS FROM REDEEMEDREADER.COM

The Reading Challenge for Kids will get you and your child reading a broader variety of books this year and perhaps discovering new favorites. This reading challenge is adapted by us and used with permission from the fine folks at RedeemedReader.com Check out their website for more information about this reading challenge, and for great book reviews and book suggestions for your kids.

Reading or Not

At this grade level, it is entirely appropriate that most of these books be read-alouds and picture books. In fact, many sources recommend that parents continue reading to their children well past the time their children become accomplished readers.

How Long Do We Count Picture Books?

I recently heard this beautiful quote from Sarah Mackenzie at the Read-Aloud Revival:

"Another thing I want to point out is picture books. As your child grows older, do not stop reading picture books. Picture books are written, often times, with more eloquent, beautiful language than chapter books or middle grade novels so the reading level in the picture book is actually higher than it is in the novel. A beautifully written picture book is like poetry and an art gallery combined into one. So they are not less-than, or they're not inferior to longer novels. The beautiful thing about picture books is because they're short, you can experience more stories this way. So if you prioritize picture books over novels when it comes to reading aloud, you will actually fill your child's memories and childhood with more stories..." (Hear the whole conversation on the Read-Aloud Revival podcast, at the beginning of episode 121.)

How It Works

On the following pages, you'll find four lists of books which you are meant to read one after another this year. Not all families will make it through all the lists, so you will need to choose a reading goal early in the year and set your pace accordingly.

The Light Reader plan has 13 books, which sets a pace of 1 book every four weeks. The majority of families can and should do at least this much.

The Avid Reader plan adds another 13 books, which increases the pace to 1 book every two weeks. This is doable for most families.

The Committed Reader plan adds a further 26 books,

bringing the total to 52, or 1 book every week. By including picture books, we think that even this faster pace is not too rigorous, suitable for enthusiastic readers with time in their schedules.

The Obsessed Reader plan doubles the total yet again, bringing it to 104 books, which sets a pace of 2 books every week. We highly recommend this challenge, but it may be too intense for families with already-packed schedules!

Getting Started

Begin with the Light plan, which includes suggestions for 13 books. Choose those books and read them in any order, checking them off as you complete them.

Next, advance to the Avid plan, using the criteria there to choose another 13 books and read them in any order.

Then it's time to move to the Committed plan with a further 26 books, again reading them in any order.

If you have completed the Committed plan (that's 52 books so far!), you are ready to brave the Obsessed plan.

If you want to finish your books in a school year rather than in an entire calendar year, the timeline shifts a bit, so be sure to set your goal at the beginning of the year and pace yourself accordingly.

Here's the pace for a 36-week schedule:

Light Reader: One book every two to three weeks.

Avid Reader: One book every week or two.

Committed Reader: One and a half books every week.

Obsessed Reader: Almost three books every week.

But I Don't Have Any Idea Which Books to Choose!

We have your back! Beginning on page 80 you'll find hundreds of book ideas you'll love this year.

If you want more ideas, we highly recommend your local librarian, the Read-Aloud Revival podcast, and the Timberdoodle Facebook groups as excellent starting points. It's also a wonderful idea to peek at the additional reading ideas in the Story of the World Activity Book.

Will This Be Expensive?

It doesn't need to be. You can read library books and e-versions, buy used, borrow from friends, and scour your family bookshelves. Don't forget that many libraries have free e-versions, as well. It doesn't get much more convenient than that!

But How Do I Fit This Much Reading Into My Day?

Here are eight ideas to incorporate more reading into your family's busy schedule and unique schooling style:

1. Focus on Picture Books

Picture books allow for more stories in less time, but don't lack at all for impact. If time will be an issue this year, or if you're also wrangling younger children who aren't yet ready for pictureless reading, just plan now that this year will be The Year of Picture Books and embrace it!

2. Assign Independent Reading

This becomes more and more feasible as your child's reading skills improve, but even now he can read some books independently, and it would be wise to incorporate that into your routine. This can be done in conjunction with quiet time or simply throughout the day. Our household often uses it as a strategy to calm the hyper and soothe the sad—I need you to go read one book and then come back and we'll try again.

3. Quiet Time!

Does your family implement a quiet time already? Reading is a natural perk for that time, especially if you help your child find all his favorite books and make them particularly accessible for this time slot. (We've been known to use a laundry basket filled with books!) Quiet time can be as simple as setting a timer for 30 minutes (or more) and having your child sit with his favorite blanket, weighted lap pad, or stuffed animal to read. Since he may not yet be reading entire books independently, this is a great time for picture books or familiar stories, and it sets the tone for years to come. If it's possible for you to grab a book that you've been wanting to read and embrace the same plan, you'll be modeling what an ageless wonder reading can be. Of course, if your household is filled with little ones, it may be more practical to use this time for feeding babies or fixing dinner and there's no shame in that, but consider your options as you plan your year.

4. Sneak Reading Into Your Existing Routines

What routines are already going well for you? Could you incorporate a reading time right into your existing bedtime routine, family devotions, car time, snack time, or other routine?

5. Audiobooks

Incorporate audiobooks and save the designated reader some time and energy. This is a particularly spectacular move for car time, art time, or puzzle time.

6. Put Busy Fingers to Work

Encourage quiet activities such as puzzles, Plus-Plus, or coloring while you read aloud or play the audiobook. It can be legitimately impossible for your kinesthetic learner to sit perfectly still and listen angelically, but break out the "listening time only" tools and suddenly everyone looks forward to reading!

7. Brothers and Sisters

You don't have to be the only one reading to your child. Have an older sibling read to your second-grader as part of their school lessons. The older sibling will gain fluency as your second-grader soaks up the one-on-one time. Your second-grader is also old enough to read books to his younger siblings, and it's the sweetest thing to watch! (No younger ones in your home? How about cousins, playmates, or even the family pet?)

8. Grandpa, Grandma, Aunties, Oh My!

Perhaps an auntie would welcome the opportunity to have Friday evenings be read-aloud time, complete with hot cocoa and scones. Or Grandma might love the idea of hosting all of her grandchildren once a month for a giant book party—each

child could bring his favorite book to be enjoyed by all. Too far away? Grandpa could record his favorite book (any audio-recording app should work), then send the book to your child so that he can read along with Grandpa.

Let's Read!

Pick your plan, choose some books with your child, and get started!

THE LIGHT READER

The Challenge	The Book You Chose	Date Completed
1. A book about being a Christian or about what the Bible teaches	THE BIGGEST STORY	9|17
2. A book about the world	USBORNE - MY FIRST WORLD	9|16
3. A biography	THE STORY OF RUBY BRIDGES	9|3
4. A classic novel/story	CHARLOTTES WEB	9|20
5. A book your grandparent (or other relative) says was his/her favorite at your age	HAROLD & THE PURPLE CRAYON	10|12
6. A book from the Old Testament (or a retelling of an Old Testament story)	THE BOOK OF JONAH	9|30
7. A book from the New Testament (or a retelling of a New Testament story)	THOUGHTS TO MAKE YOUR HEART SING	7|1
8. A book based on a true story	LUCKY DUCKLINGS	9|18
9. A book your pastor or Sunday School teacher recommends	INDESCRIBABLE	4|1
10. A book more than 100 years old	RAGGEDY ANN & ANDY	3|4
11. A book about families	THE LITTLE BRUTE FAMILY	9|23
12. A book about relationships or friendship	ONE COOL FRIEND	10|23
13. A book featuring someone of a different ethnicity than you	FLY HIGH! BESSIE COLEMAN	9|20
	THE OTHER SIDE	11|14

The Challenge	The Book You Chose	Date Completed
14. A book about someone who came from another country	ALL THE WAY TO AMERICA	9/18
15. A book of fairy tales or folk tales (or an extended retelling of one)	PRINCESS & THE PEA	9/18
16. A book recommended by a parent or sibling	IF YOU'LL BE MY VALENTINE	2/11
17. A book by or about a missionary	MOTHER THERSEA	11/14
18. A Caldecott, Newbery, or Geisel Award winner	LION & THE MOUSE	9/23
19. A book about a holiday	TWAS THE NIGHT BEFORE CHRISTMAS	12/22
20. A book about grandparents	NO KIM CHI FOR ME! DEAR JUNO	9/23
21. A book with visual puzzles	THE CIRCUS SHIP	9/23
22. A book that has a fruit of the Spirit in its title	SOMEONE LOVES YOU, MR HATCH	10/6
23. A book about a farm	FARMER DUCK DUCK TO RESCUE	10/6
24. A book about illness or medicine	FLORENCE NICHTEN GALE	10/7
25. A book about school or learning	THIS IS MY HOME, THIS IS MY SCHOOL	10/6
26. A graphic novel	THE LOST TRAIL	9/13

The Challenge	The Book You Chose	Date Completed
27. A book of poetry	THE LLAMA W/ NO PAJAMA	10/7
28. A book with a great cover	ROBIN HOOD	10/1
29. A book about food	BEST CHEF IN 2ND GRADE	11/14
30. A book about weather	THUNDER CAKE	10/7
31. A book about an adventure	MAC B. KID SPIES	1/26
32. A book by or about William Shakespeare (or a retelling of one of his plays)	BARD OF AVON	11/14
33. A funny book	RICHARD SCARRY - FUNNIEST STORY	1130
34. A mystery or detective story	ZACH & ZOE	1/24
35. An easy reader classic (e.g., A Bargain for Frances, Frog and Toad, Little Bear, etc.)	OH THE PLACES YOU'LL GO	1/2
36. A book by or about a famous American	BEFORE SHE WAS HARRIET	1/23
37. A book about ancient history	USBORNE BOOK OF WORLD HISTORY	9/28
38. A book about medieval history	CASTLE	3/5
39. A book about money	ALEXANDER WHO USED TO BE RICH	1/26

www.timberdoodle.com • ©2019

The Challenge	The Book You Chose	Date Completed
40. A book about art or artists	THE CHALK BOX KID	9123
41. A book about music or a musician	MOLE MUSIC	315
42. A book about an invention or inventor	BALLOONS OVER BROADWAY	1113
43. A book about feelings or emotions	JABARI JUMPS	9118
44. A book about a boy	MY FATHER'S DRAGON	2116
45. A book about a girl	NANCY CLANCY	
46. A book about books or a library	THAT BOOK WOMAN	2111
47. A book about adoption	THE DAY OF YOUR ARRIVAL	1126
48. A book about someone who is differently abled (blind, deaf, mentally handicapped, etc.)	JUST BECAUSE	316
49. A book you or your family owns but you've never read	LIFE OF AN EARTH WORM	6115
50. A book about babies	MOON BABIES	1129
51. A book about writing	HOME WORK	212
52. A book made into a movie (but read the book first!)	CHARLOTTE'S WEB	9123

The Challenge	The Book You Chose	Date Completed
53. A book about prayer	IMAGES OF GOD	2/6
54. A book recommended by a librarian or teacher	A GUIDE TO GRANDMA & GRANDPA	7/2
55. An encyclopedia, dictionary or almanac	USBORNE'S CHILDS ENCYCLOPEDIA	10/2
56. A book about building or architecture	LOOK AT THAT BUILDING	3/4
57. A biography of a world leader	TO DARE MIGHTY THINGS	2/12
58. A book published the same year you (the student) were born	EXTRA YARN	2/11
59. A book with a one-word title	POND	3/5
60. A book about service	THE GIVING TREE	10/9
61. A book about siblings	LOUISE LOVES ART	3/17
62. A book about animals	GROUNDHOG DAY	2/6
63. A book featuring a dog	BIG DOG LITTLE DOG	1/29
64. A book featuring a cat	MILLIONS OF CATS	3/6
65. A wordless book	HAROLD & THE PURPLE CRAYON	10/3
66. A book about plants or gardening	KARL, GET OUT OF THE GARDEN	9/30
67. A book about a hobby or skill you want to learn	BEAR GRYLLS SURVIVAL	5/17
68. A book of comics	CALVIN & HOBBS	3/11
69. A book about a famous war	CIVIL WAR ON SUNDAY	3/13
70. A book about sports	FROG PLAYS T-BALL	4/26
71. A book about math (numbers, mathematicians, patterns…)	ONE GRAIN OF RICE	6/16
72. A book about suffering or poverty	THE HUNDRED DRESSES	
73. A book by your favorite author	A LIGHT IN THE ATTIC	1/3
74. A book you've read before	MAGNIFICENT THING	6/16
75. A book with an ugly cover		
76. A Christian novel		
77. A book about travel or transportation	LETS GO FOR A DRIVE	8/10
78. A book about the natural world	THE BOY WHO DREW BIRDS	1/4

The Challenge	The Book You Chose	Date Completed
79. A biography of an author	A MOUSE, A BOY & A SPIDER	3-1-1
80. A book published in 2019-2020	JUST ASK	
81. A historical fiction book	THE WHIPPING BOY	3/16
82. A book about science or a scientist	INDESCRIBABLE	9/23
83. A book about safety or survival	OFFICER GLORIA & BUCKLE	3/12
84. A book about space or an astronaut	100 THINGS ABOUT SPACE	5/7
85. A book set in Central or South America	WAITING FOR BIBLIO BURRO	
86. A book set in Africa	UN COMMON TRAVELER	3/4
87. A book set in Asia	RED BUTTERFLY TIKI TIKI	2/3
88. A book set in Europe	A WALK IN LONDON	11/13
89. A book with a color in its title	WE'LL PAINT THE OCTOPUS RED	3/10
90. A book about manners	MIND YOUR MANNERS B.B. WOLF	3/6
91. A book about spring	COME NEXT SEASON	2/13
92. A book about summer	ICE CREAM SUMMER	2/28
93. A book about autumn	AUTUM EQUINOX - CELEBRATE	10/2
94. A book about winter	WINTER CAKE	2/8
95. A book from the 0-100 Dewey Decimal section of your library	IMAGES OF GOD	
96. A book from the 100-200 Dewey Decimal section of your library	HOW TO CODE #1	2/6
97. A book from the 200-300 Dewey Decimal section of your library	LET THE WHOLE EARTH SING PRAISE	2/3
98. A book from the 300-400 Dewey Decimal section of your library	VOTE!	2/3
99. A book from the 400-500 Dewey Decimal section of your library	100 FIRST WORDS IN SPANISH	
100. A book from the 500-600 Dewey Decimal section of your library	BIG BOOK OF BUGS	
101. 600 - ~~700~~	STATE COOK BOOK	1/30
102. ~~600~~ 700	A GIRLS GUIDE - HOW TO BE GOOD @	6/18
103. 800	☞ A STAGE FULL OF SHAKESPEARE	6/26
104. 900	MARS	2/17

BEGINNING READING, WRITING, SPELLING, AND STORIES

This year your child will progress a long way in his reading abilities. Watch for 16 new phonograms, including OA, IGH, KN, and others. Hands-on activities continue to provide a tactile way to review and learn words, while 25 exciting decodable stories help increase comprehension.

Spelling You See is a magnificent way to reinforce the phonics you're studying in All About Reading, in just 10 minutes a day.

With 6-Trait Writing your child will begin to develop into a skilled writer using short and engaging lessons.

Finally, My First Story Writing Book includes all kinds of fascinating writing assignments to complete in the very colorful book. Your child will design a book cover, imagine what a given character would say, and so much more.

OH, YAY! READING!

YES, IT'S ESSENTIAL. LET'S ALSO MAKE IT FUN!

Helping a child develop into a fully competent and eager reader has been the highlight of many a teaching parent! In fact, encouraging reading skills is one of your biggest goals this year. So how do you facilitate that?

1) Make It Rewarding
Whether he is a natural reader or one who will take a few years to fully master this skill, it is critical to make reading as fun and rewarding as possible now. Reading is naturally exciting, so all you are going to need to do is allow him to experience this thrill himself! As you know, one of the simplest, most universally appealing techniques is to get him reading "real books" in his areas of interest just as much as possible. Use the readers included, but also supplement with library books that suit his interests and current skill. The reading challenge lends itself to this as there is so much flexibility in the titles you choose.

2) Read Together
Just because he's beginning to read doesn't mean that his literature intake should be limited to phonetic books. Foster his love of literature by frequently reading books aloud that interest him and discussing them together, just as you've been doing.

3) Write Slowly
Take a good look at your child's abilities and writing readiness before insisting that he complete all of the written lessons we've included as they are designed. Some children develop their fine motor skills more slowly than others and those children benefit most from scaffolding the writing they need to do, not from suddenly increasing it above their skill level.

Here are the writing assignments you can anticipate this year:

Spelling You See
I'd prioritize this as the most important that your student writes himself since those motor movements are what will help him retain the phonics he's learning. It's designed to only be used for 10 minutes a day, so even a struggling writer will be able to see light at the end of the tunnel and persist.

Daily 6-Trait Writing
Add this one in next—it doesn't start until the 12th week of school, so it gives him some time to build skills.

My First Story Writing Book
This book packs a big impact for a small amount of writing, and it boasts high-interest activities on each page. Try it and see how he does. If you end up saving it for next year, there's no harm done!

Of course, if he's ready for the content but not the writing on the last two, you could sign yourself up as scribe for the day and write down the answers he dictates for you!

ALL ABOUT READING

BASIC ~ COMPLETE ~ ELITE

The backbone of this year's language arts is All About Reading, the multisensory, mastery-based program that you've been hearing so much about. Suitable for all learning styles, AAR teaches phonics, decoding, fluency, and comprehension in a fun and engaging way.

Moving at a gentler pace than other more intense reading programs, with AAR only one new concept is taught at a time. Their precept-upon-precept program works with almost all students, and AAR's built-in review system helps learning to stick.

You will be thrilled to know that no prior training is needed; AAR has lightly scripted and illustrated "open and go" lessons that make your job easy and stress-free!

It may be helpful to note, though, that there is often a small amount of physical prep-work needed for the lessons. For instance, cutting apart the flashcards, prepping the game, or grabbing the glue for your child. What you don't need to do is struggle to understand the lesson, then repeat it in second-grader-friendly terms. That's already done for you!

The now full-color student activity books provide the meat of the lessons. Your child will be swimming fish through an underwater castle, reading practice sentences, using paper pickles as a syllable tag, and so much more.

You'll also be using both phonetic readers this year. Frankly, these are the best readers we have ever seen — beautifully illustrated hardcover books with finely detailed, full-color drawings; easily advancing text; and ever-so-funny-to-second-graders storylines. From the persistent train cat in the first chapter, to Britches the sheep's funny fears about shearing, both parents and children will enjoy the amusing, wholesome stories and illustrations.

All About Reading Level 3 picks up from where your student left off in Level 2, adding new skills systematically. Many hands-on activities continue to make learning and review engaging for students, while the 25 decodable short stories

with comprehension activities take Level 3 above and beyond.

There is a convenient pretest in the beginning of the teacher's manual to make sure your child is at the most-appropriate grade level. If this is your first year homeschooling and you find you need to start with an earlier level, please don't be discouraged. The results you'll get from going back and starting where he actually needs to be will be so worth the time spent!

What About the App?

While physical letter tiles are included in our standard kits, some busy families will find the continual sifting, sorting, and set-up to be a bit overwhelming. For you we'd suggest that you consider using the app, which does all of that for you.

Just select the lesson you are currently teaching and the appropriate letter tiles for that lesson will appear in their proper configuration, making it easy for you to teach and easy for your child to learn.

Look for the Letter Tiles app, available separately on iTunes, Google Play, and the Kindle app store.

Scheduling

There are 54 lessons in all, so conventional scheduling would lead you to believe that completing 1.5 lessons a week is best. However, All About Reading strongly encourages you to pace yourself to the child, not the program. Isn't that a relief? They suggest simply completing 20 minutes of All About Reading time each day, knowing that some days lessons will fly by, and other days you'll want to spend more time on a concept.

SPELLING YOU SEE

BASIC ~ COMPLETE ~ ELITE

This multisensory spelling program will help your child become a confident, successful speller, naturally and at his own speed. Because Spelling You See encourages visual memory rather than rote memory, there are no weekly spelling lists or tests and very little instructor preparation. Each daily lesson in Spelling You See: Wild Tales uses real words presented in context within nursery rhymes and interesting nonfiction passages about animals.

Spelling You See: Wild Tales is colorful, short, to the point, and fun!

You may notice that this is your only handwriting course this year. While the publisher would advocate adding a separate workbook for handwriting, we feel that most second-graders will find that their kits include plenty of writing for one year. Your child is still developing his fine motor skills and his attention span, and allowing those skills to develop naturally will be much more appealing to both of you!

Scheduling
The 36 weeks of work, with five daily activities each week, are already planned out for you. Just open and go!

A COUPLE THOUGHTS:
Ideally you will not complete more than one short spelling lesson every day for best retention. If your student is at all overwhelmed by the lesson length, keep in mind that there is enough work in each lesson to teach a speedy writer, but a more methodical writer could be overwhelmed trying to complete it all. Consider starting a timer for 10 to 15 minutes when you begin the day's work, and stop where you are when it rings. The next day, just move on to the new lesson.

Also, if you're using a four-day week or otherwise don't get to all five days of work in a week, it is expected that you will still count that lesson as complete at the end of the week and move to the next one.

6-TRAIT WRITING

BASIC ~ COMPLETE ~ ELITE

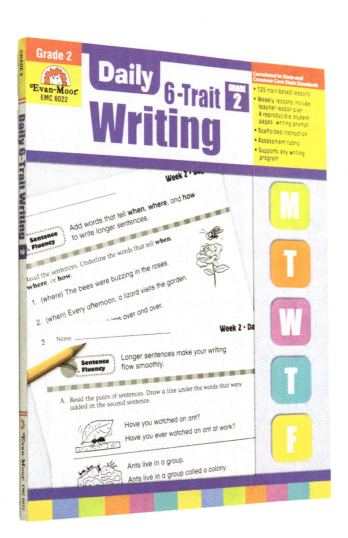

Are you familiar with trait writing? Trait-based writing is an impressive method educators have developed to determine if a child's writing is skilled or not.

The six traits or characteristics that shape quality writing are content; organization; word choice; sentence fluency; voice; and conventions, which include grammar, spelling, and mechanics. It may sound ominous, but Daily 6-Trait Writing has made it effortless.

These short daily assignments are designed to build skills without being overwhelming. We love them for their brevity, but also because they are so thorough!

Scheduling

Designed for one short lesson a day, ending after 25 weeks of school. We suggest starting this after 11 weeks of school to make sure your student is ready. Or, if you prefer, you could begin immediately and only do three to four days' work each week so that you don't finish too early.

If you have a student who struggles with fine motor skills, you may have more success if you completely separate writing skills from motor skills. Most families do this by allowing their students to dictate their writing, but you could also use a whiteboard (bigger writing may be easier) or allow your student to use a computer or tablet/phone. That allows your child to build fantastic writing skills, even while his motor skills are still developing.

MY FIRST STORY WRITING BOOK

~~BASIC~~ COMPLETE ~ ELITE

This lovely write-in book is for the beginning novelist who needs or longs to learn to write stories but doesn't know where to start. My First Story Writing Book is packed with peculiar people and unusual locations to jumpstart your child's imagination.

My First Story Writing Book takes your young writer through each part of story writing, showing him how to create characters, develop plot lines, and design dramatic twists.

With fun activities including word games, "story mazes" with ideas for plot twists, and writing diary entries for characters, as well as plenty of tips on writing descriptively, My First Story Writing Book will kindle your child's imagination.

Side note: Story writing may not strike you as a valuable skill for a non-author at first glance, yet it is. A lawyer must tell a compelling story to demonstrate why his client is right. A doctor tells a clear story to explain how this surgery will work. An EMT documents a patient's story to assist with treatment in the ER. Farmers sell the most if they can offer a compelling story of their farm... and on and on it goes. Not to mention all the times parents are called upon to tell a story or explain a family rule!

Scheduling

Plan to have your child complete one activity a week. Allowing additional time for any particularly difficult assignments, this schedule should still allow you to complete the book in a school year. Or, if you prefer, it can make a lovely, fast-paced summer activity book, especially if you aim to complete an activity a day.

WORD FUN

~~BASIC~~ ~~COMPLETE~~ **ELITE**

Written in a whimsical and conversational manner, Word Fun is a gentle introduction to parts of speech. The goofy storylines and striking, full-of-movement illustrations in Word Fun make what would otherwise be a dull topic inviting.

Word Fun teaches the eight most significant parts of speech: nouns, verbs, adjectives, adverbs, pronouns, conjunctions, interjections, and prepositions.

Each is presented in an "If you were a _, you could _." fashion, making the concepts so much more memorable than a textbook definition.

Scheduling

Scheduling is flexible; we suggest covering one of the eight parts of speech every week, putting you through the entire book four times this year. However, if your child is already comfortable with each one and its name and role you may wish to drop back to one a month or just straight through once.

LOST TRAIL

~~BASIC~~ ~~COMPLETE~~ **ELITE**

Many families have found that graphic novels provide huge incentives to their budding readers. We've included a favorite true story; try it with your child and see if he enjoys it. Just so you know, this book is written at a level that most second-graders will find challenging but, by the end of the year, quite doable.

Lost on a Mountain in Maine

In 1939 the entire nation anxiously watched as a parent's nightmare unfolded. Twelve-year-old Donn Fendler was hiking Maine's highest mountain, mile-high Katahdin, when he became separated from his family. As a dark storm moved in, Donn became even more disoriented. He emerged nine long days later, grossly malnourished, bare feet cut to shreds, and with scarcely a stitch of clothing intact, but alive.

Lost Trail: Nine Days Alone in the Wilderness is the true story of that perilous journey, meticulously retold in a graphic novel.

Now Told in a Gripping Graphic Novel

Donn's gripping story was made famous 70 years ago by the best-selling book, Lost on a Mountain in Maine. Now, for the first time Donn tells the story of survival and rescue from his own perspective in this skillfully illustrated graphic novel, Lost Trail.

He Survived Nine Days of Cold, Hunger, Bears, and More

Children will be enthralled to read the day-by-day account of how a 12-year-old Boy Scout from a New York City suburb survived cold, hunger, bears, a tumble into an icy river, and hallucinations. They will cheer to read of how Donn's rescue was celebrated with a huge parade and an opportunity to meet the President of the United States. As a graphic novel, Lost Trail introduces younger and more reluctant readers to a true story that has captivated children for more than 70 years.

Scheduling

We suggest not assigning this book, but turning your child loose with it as soon as his reading ability allows. If that doesn't work well for him, consider assigning 10 minutes of reading twice a week (or two pages a week, which will take him through in a school year).

Note!

This book shows an imaginary monster that plagued Donn's mind. You will want to discuss this with your child, or even cover it up if your second-grader would find it too scary.

HANDS-ON MATH

Basic math is a critical skill for your child to master, whether he grows up to be a carpenter, doctor, accountant, or farmer. But all too often math programs rely on memorization instead of comprehension, leaving the student at a disadvantage.

That's not going to happen to your child! The real-world math problems posed in Math-U-See (combined with the hands-on manipulatives) create an unbeatable math program.

The Math-U-See manipulatives are a versatile workhorse. Not only are they integral to the curriculum, they also facilitate a depth of mathematical awareness in freeplay and fun, experimental activities.

By using the Math-U-See manipulative blocks, your child will more easily grasp that a one-unit block plus a nine-unit block equals a ten-unit block. And that's before you even crack open the textbooks!

MATH-U-SEE BETA

BASIC ~ COMPLETE ~ ELITE

Math-U-See will take your child beyond mere rote memorization by using step-by-step problem solving until your child is able to reason his way through the mathematical problem. Concepts are mastered, not spiraled, to ensure greater comprehension.

Unlike our other math programs, Math-U-See does require a fair amount of parental involvement. At first glance it can seem overwhelming. But they have bent over backwards to make the lesson planning as painless as possible. Still, at this grade, feel free to merely skim the teacher's guide, as it is pretty straightforward.

The Math-U-See supplemental DVD (and teacher's guide, when you wish to use it) will teach you, the parent, more than just how to solve a math problem. It will also show why the problem is solved in this manner and when to apply the concept. DVDs can be played on a DVD player or computer; however, Windows 10 users will need to download a separate video player.

Some parents prefer to watch the lessons themselves and then teach their students personally, while most prefer to watch alongside their students, pausing the video, rewinding, and clarifying as needed.

After watching the

video lesson or your recreated lesson, your student can practice the concept for three pages, review the new concept alongside cumulative older concepts, and finally complete a "test" page to show that he has mastered the knowledge and is ready for the next week's lesson.

Your child may not need to complete every one of these pages. At risk of over-simplifying, the practice worksheets (A, B, C) are to be used with the manipulatives until your child reaches an "aha!" moment and grasps the lesson. He may then move to the review pages (D, E, F) and should at least complete worksheet D in its entirety. If he's breezing through the pages, you have several great options, including having him do every other problem, or skip E or F or both. (You do want to be sure he's not rusty on any of those problems before skipping, though—many students will do best completing all or most of the worksheets.) Worksheet G is often a test, application question, or extra-credit work. It's okay to skip, but valuable to complete.

Scheduling

Plan on one lesson a week, with up to seven double-sided worksheets, to complete this in a school year. That builds in a buffer of six weeks so that if your child needs a slower pace or if illness or vacations necessitate time off, you will still finish on schedule.

TENZI GAME

BASIC ~ **COMPLETE ~ ELITE**

Simple, fast, fun, and purposeful, Tenzi is a perfect addition to your child's curriculum. This is drillwork that doesn't feel at all like drillwork!

In the original Tenzi game, players roll 10 dice and reroll those that don't match until all 10 display identical numbers.

Tenzi requires fast hands, the ability to make accurate calculations, and the gift of laughter.

As wonderful as Tenzi is, after a while you may find playing the same game becomes tedious. But with 77 Ways to Play Tenzi, you will find a number of creative ways to make this dice game interesting. Each durable, oversized card has instructions for a unique game. Draw a new card each round, call for rematches, or even mix and match to create complicated rounds. There are three types of games: score-keeping games, non-speed games, and pattern games. In the pattern games, you arrange the dice to match the card, which adds an additional layer of educational value and is spectacular for developing logic, as well as spatial puzzle solving.

Not all of the colorful cards in 77 Ways to Play Tenzi will be equally appealing, but changing up the game greatly increases the replay value. Three of the 77 cards are blank, so create your own Tenzi game and name it after yourself!

Scheduling

Plan to break out the Tenzi game and card deck at least once a week, and either play a competitive game together or let your child race himself.

THIS IS AS CRITICAL AS IT IS APPEALING

In Timberdoodle's curriculum kits, you will find a rigorous pursuit of thinking skills for every child, in every grade. This is simply not an optional skill for your child. A child who can think logically will be able to learn well and teach himself logically in ways that an untrained brain will find difficult.

Be thankful that you won't have to persuade your child to learn to think, though – he's wired for problem solving and has been learning from the moment his eyes first saw you. We're guessing this portion of the curriculum will be the hardest not to race through. After all, who doesn't want to fill in the blanks for a logic puzzle, help the squirrels store their acorns, or flip the cubes to match the picture?

BUILDING THINKING SKILLS 1

BASIC ~ COMPLETE ~ ELITE

This series of thinking-skills books is among our favorites because of their tremendous scope. Studies have shown that students using these books have raised their national test scores significantly in both content and cognitive tests. Not many curricula have been that thoroughly tested.

In this volume your child will develop four basic analytical skills (similarities/differences, sequences, classification, and analogies) through both figural and verbal problems. In addition, there are problems dealing with deductive reasoning, map skills, Venn diagrams, mental manipulation of two-dimensional objects, and much more.

Does that sound overwhelming? Don't worry, it truly isn't. When I was a child, these are the types of puzzles and pages that were often a highlight of the day.

You'll simply work from front to back in the book, studying one skill at a time and building on it. Pages are perforated, perfect if your student would be overwhelmed by the scope of the course and would do better if he were simply handed this week's pages.

A note about the writing: Some pages do expect a fair amount of writing from your student. If this is hindering your student rather than helping him, feel free to have him type his answers, answer orally, or dictate as you write them in. While writing does strengthen brain connections, this is a thinking skills course, not a writing course, and we don't want him to be held back from a full enjoyment of thinking skills while he's gaining the dexterity needed for writing.

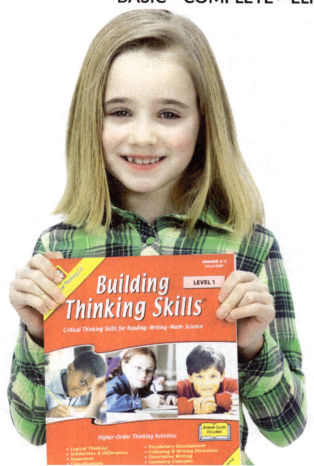

Scheduling

Completing nine pages a week will get you through the entire book in a year. Most children will love that pace, but if it is too much for your student, feel free to drop that back to four to five pages a week and work through it in two years.

SQUIRRELS GO NUTS

~~BASIC~~ **COMPLETE ~ ELITE**

What looks like a simple sliding game is anything but simple. Squirrels Go Nuts will have your child sliding the pieces along the grooves of the gameboard trying to avoid dropping the nuts into the wrong hole.

He may begin trying to solve the Squirrels Go Nuts challenges by moving the pieces randomly, but he will soon discover the logic behind the game. By analyzing the position of the holes and acorns, he will discover which squirrel can fill which hole and in which order to move the squirrels. When all the nuts are in a hole, the challenge is complete.

With challenges ranging from easy to more difficult, Squirrels Go Nuts is a fun, attractive logic-building game for the entire family—if your second-grader is willing to share!

As the manufacturer notes, the small metal ball inside every acorn is to avoid having the acorn bounce too much when it drops on the floor. This makes it ever so much easier to retrieve. Thankfully, if you loose more than one nut, you can replace them with small marbles or pay shipping to order replacements directly from Smart Games.

Scheduling
Plan on 1 to 2 challenges a week to complete all 60 this year. Of course, your eager beaver is always welcome to retry previous puzzles and see if he can do it again, but with fewer moves.

Q-BITZ SOLO

~~BASIC~~ ~~COMPLETE~~ **ELITE**

Q-bitz is a magnificent visual agility game that will never lose its fascination. With 20 pattern cards and 16 cubes, players recreate the patterns as quickly as possible by rotating the cubes into position.

These wooden cubes fit neatly into the wooden tray, making a pleasant-to-the-touch visual perception challenge.

While it could be used as a creative mosaic, we've included it specifically for the visual perceptual skills it teaches. Visual perception training has never been this engaging!

Scheduling

With 20 cards, we suggest doing 2 every week. For the first time through, simply have your student replicate the pattern on each of the cards, writing down how long it takes him.

On the next time through, he can either try to beat his last time or he can try the rolling technique. To play that way he will roll all his cubes onto the table, then place as many as he can using only the face-up side. Next, he will roll the remaining cubes again, and repeat. This strengthens visual processing even more, as he has to compare the openings on his board to the face-up cubes and the pattern card.

On his final time through, let him study each card for 10 seconds (or whatever is a fair time for him), then flip the card over and see how much he can recreate from memory! The game allows for up to two peeks, as needed, but challenge him to work his visual memory as best he can. (One way to do that would be to have him place all the cubes before peeking, even if he isn't sure of their placement. He then takes a look and makes a mental note of the pieces he needs to remove and fix. The card is flipped back over, and he tries again...)

WHO DISCOVERED CHOCOLATE?

Many history curriculum options make the mistake of focusing solely on U.S.A. history. As important as that is, doesn't it make more sense to start with the big picture of history? This year you'll learn about the Middle Ages, covering the major historical events in the years 400 – 1,600, from the fall of Rome to the rise of the Renaissance. You'll answer questions like:

What happened to the Giant Fovor of the Mighty Blows?
Why did the Ottoman Turks drag their war ships across dry land?
And, of course, who discovered chocolate?

Geography this year will be equally intriguing as you read the fascinating and attractive book, This Is the World, by classic author-illustrator M. Sasek. Additionally, complete the vibrant pages of Skill Sharpeners Geography to master important geography concepts.

With Famous Figures of the Renaissance, you'll find that history becomes hands-on as you assemble movable figures of 10 of the key characters of the Renaissance, from Martin Luther to Isabella I.

This is very easy to use. Just read your child one chapter from the story book, then ask him to tell you what it was about. Afterward, pick an activity page or worksheet that is appropriate for your child's interest and your schedule.

If this is your first year teaching history it is worth noting that

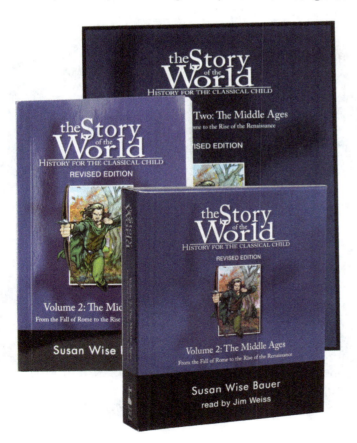

some second-graders will initially have trouble staying tuned in for Story of the World. If that's your child, check out the auditory processing tips on page 66.

Did you see how big the activity book is? Keep in mind that one of its biggest advantages is the fact that it offers a wide range of activities for each lesson. Pick the ones that best fit your child's learning style and your family's schedule, but don't try to do them all!

Scheduling

Completing three chapters every two weeks is a realistic pace that will get you through the books in just under a year. If you purchased the Elite kit, you'll love having the audio book. It includes the same content as the story book, but it can be much more convenient. Just pop in the CD and listen to your history with your child while you're driving, cooking, feeding the baby, or any of the myriad other activities that keep your hands too busy to hold a book.

Note: Please do not consider this series a Providential view of history which recognizes God's hand in history, but rather a history text that attempts to include all significant historical and cultural accounts. Where you find details with Biblical references that are inaccurate because of sparseness, use this opportunity to interject more of His story. Simply skip anything that is uncomfortable for your family. These are very minor issues that are easily addressed and shouldn't keep you from this overall excellent program.

SKILL SHARPENERS GEOGRAPHY

~~BASIC~~ ~ **COMPLETE ~ ELITE**

Skill Sharpeners Geography lets your child explore his world while learning key map skills and geography concepts with little fuss on your part. The cross-curricular activities integrate the most current geography standards, and each eye-catching book is divided into colorful collections of engaging, grade-appropriate themes.

Each theme includes short nonfiction reading selections, comprehension questions, vocabulary practice, and writing prompts.

Optional hands-on activities will excite the kinesthetic child in your home. To use them you'll need a few common tools, like scissors, glue, tape, and coloring materials. It may also be helpful to note that there are a couple of activities (pages 69 and 79 in Skill Sharpeners Geography) which suggest that you first glue the pieces together and then color the scene. In our opinion, it would at least be worth considering whether to have your child color first, and then cut those pieces out. For some kids, that would be less frustrating than coloring on top of glued paper.

Skill Sharpeners Geography takes your child beyond just the basics of geography and includes a smattering of histories and cultures within our world. The colorful illustrations and pages will grab your child's attention, and the handy

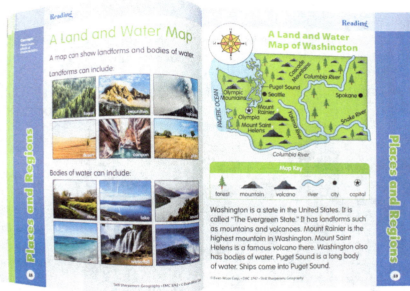

(removable) answer key in the back allows you to help your student to easily check his work.

Scheduling

Instead of going by actual page count (132), it makes more sense to split up the work by activity pages. So each week you'll want to complete any instructional pages needed as well as about 2 of the 65 activities.

And yes, you may truly skip the activity pages (with no guilt) if that isn't how your child learns best. In that case, plan on 4 pages a week, including the skipped activity pages.

~~BASIC COMPLETE~~ **ELITE**

With Famous Figures of the Renaissance, you'll find that history becomes hands-on as you assemble movable figures of 10 of the key characters of old, such as Christopher Columbus or William Shakespeare.

While listening to The Story of the World, your avid artist can color in the detailed figures. A hole punch and common fasteners will allow their arms and legs to move and their swords and shields to flash.

For the meticulous child who wants it colored exactly right, matching pre-colored action figures are also included.

Don't forget about the detailed biography section in the front of the book, providing key information about the characters. A companion reading list for each figure is also included—perfect if your child wants to learn more or if you're looking for just the right book this week.

Scheduling

Aim to do one or two figures a month, or time them to match up with Story of the World as follows.

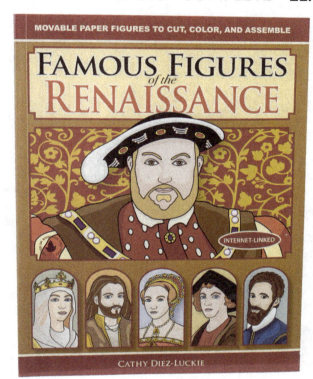

MOVABLE PAPER FIGURES TO CUT, COLOR, AND ASSEMBLE

FAMOUS FIGURES of the RENAISSANCE

INTERNET-LINKED

CATHY DIEZ-LUCKIE

1. Johannes Gutenberg: Chapter 35
2. Christopher Columbus Chapter: 31
3. Isabella I: Chapters 28 and 31
4. *Leonardo da Vinci: Chapters 27, 28, and continuing
5. *Michelangelo: Chapters 28, 31, and continuing
6. Martin Luther: Chapters 34 and 36
7. Henry VIII: Chapter 34
8. Elizabeth I: Chapters 34, 38, and 42
9. William Shakespeare: Chapter 39
10. Galileo Galilei: Chapter 37

*FYI this person is not directly spoken of in the chapter, but is part of this era.

THIS IS THE WORLD

~~BASIC~~ ~~COMPLETE~~ **ELITE**

This Is the World: A Global Treasury presents a stunning collection of drawings of some of the world's great cities and countries, yet it is also a delightfully age-appropriate children's travel book.

Talented illustrator and storyteller M. Sasek has brought to life the best of the world's major capitals and countries for young readers, encapsulating their art, architecture, music, food, and traditions.

However, this book still may present a few concerns for conservative families as various worldviews or religions from around the globe are presented or hinted at. For example, you will read about temples and icons in Greece, firecrackers to ward off evil spirits in Hong Kong, leprechauns in Ireland, and you will also find an evolution-based reference to "primitive species" living in Australia.

Despite these concerns and others like them, we think you will find this to be a lovely book to read with your child. And we strongly encourage you to discuss issues as they arise instead of ignoring them. This is homeschooling at its best.

Scheduling

There are 16 destinations in This Is the World. We suggest you study one a week, reading, discussing, and even trying to replicate some of the art. Working your way through the book twice will cement the ideas more firmly in your child's mind.

READY TO EXPERIMENT?

Science in the Ancient World covers the work of natural philosophers from about 600 BC to the early 1500s. With Science in the Ancient World, your student will use candy to demonstrate what Democritus got wrong about atoms, find out why Hippocrates thought wine should be sprinkled on bandages, and speculate about why Leonardo da Vinci used mirror writing in all of his notebooks.

Science in the Ancient World concentrates mostly on what these ancient scientists got right, but also discusses what they got wrong, because even mistakes can advance our understanding of the natural world. Students will also learn that most of the great scientists in the last half of this period were devout Christians who investigated science to learn more about God by studying His handiwork. You're going to love this!

SCIENCE IN THE ANCIENT WORLD
~~BASIC ~~ **COMPLETE ~ ELITE**

Berean Science offers students an opportunity to study science through the lens of history. Using a narrative dialogue and a Christian worldview, Berean Science teaches science chronologically, so there are vast and varied science topics in each volume.

Fairly bursting with experiments - every lesson has some sort of activity - Berean Science's strong focus on this hands-on component makes it an ideal program for the wigglers in your household.

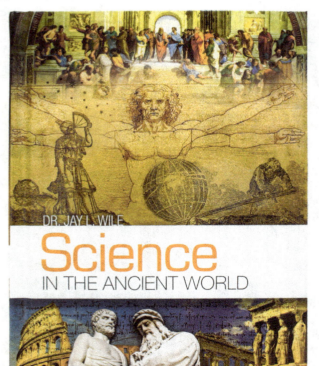

The durable hardcover textbook has lots of full-color illustrations. The lessons are concise but complete, drilling down to the core of what your child needs to know. Lesson material is often just a page or two following each activity, perfect for any child that struggles to sit and pay attention. (If that's a struggle, though, don't worry–see page 75 for tips on making strides.)

The activities, all color-coded and easy to find quickly, often involve inexpensive household items and are the gateway to the exploration of each scientific concept. Plus, each book has a helpful section in the front that tells you all the materials you will need, broken down per chapter, for doing the experiments.

Each lesson concludes with questions or additional activities for "younger," "older," and "oldest" students, so Berean Science lends itself well to multi-grade homes that prefer to use just one science curriculum for the entire family.

Lessons are taught directly from the text, so there is no cumbersome teacher's manual.

If your student appreciates beginning with notebooking pages, rather than a blank notebook, check out the free PDFs from the publisher on our website.

Scheduling
You'll notice that some of the lessons in your book are red in the index. A red lesson indicates that this lesson is optional–a bonus lesson if you will.

If you wish to only complete essential lessons, just do two lessons a week. However, if you prefer to enjoy every single lesson, you'll want to do two to three lessons a week. (In fact, if you alternate between two and three lessons, you'll come out exactly on track.)

Pro Tip:
The most intimidating part of science can be gathering the supplies required for experiments. We recommend you stop now, grab a box and the list of materials printed in the introductory pages of your textbook and collect all your needed materials, purchasing any items you need for the year on your next shopping trip. Make it more fun by considering it a full-family scavenger hunt!

Besides everyday dishware and perishable items, you should be able to collect most other items you need, and you'll never regret having already completed the most labor-intensive step of your child's science education this year.

STEM IS EVERYWHERE!

STEM learning is more than robotics and computer programming. STEM tools also include those that engage students in exploratory learning, discovery, and problem solving that teach the foundational skills of critical thinking and short- and long-term planning. So STEM includes your Me: A Compendium book as well as your Squirrels Go Nuts logic game even though they are found elsewhere in this handbook. Basically anything that goes beyond a rote read-and-regurgitate lesson undoubtedly falls into the STEM classification. In assembling this guide, many of our products could easily have been classified as STEM, but these tools seem especially appropriate for this category.

ENGINO INVENTOR

~~BASIC~~ **COMPLETE ~ ELITE**

Unlike many brick construction kits, robust Engino Inventor parts can be connected in virtually any direction or angle. Additionally, all Engino parts snap together and stay together. And with their exclusive extendable components, your child will love how easy and fast it is to build oversized simple and complex designs.

Winner of Dr. Toy's 10 Best Active Toys 2006, 10 Best Educational Toys 2007, and Best Vacation Toy 2009, Engino's easy adaptability makes it one of the best, most exciting engineering construction toys on the market.

Scheduling

Have your child build one to two models a week. Download the directions for the additional models and you'll be set for the year.

How to download the Engino instructions for the additional models:

1. Visit the Engino Instructions page, at http://www.engino.com/
From there, click "Instructions" and scroll down to the Inventor Motorized section and find the "50 models motorized set." You can choose either the 3-D instructions or the printable PDF instructions, whichever you and your child find easier to work with.

2. Alternatively, you can download the Engino Models 3-D Viewer app, available free for Android, Apple (iOs), and Windows mobile operating systems.

WILE E. COYOTE
~~BASIC~~ ~~COMPLETE~~ **ELITE**

Since 1948, Wile E. Coyote has used complex contraptions to make repeated unsuccessful attempts to catch the elusive Road Runner. This classic cartoon is known for both exaggerating and blatantly breaking the laws of physics. Now, with lighthearted text and comical illustrations, Wile E. Coyote, Physical Science Genius explains the science behind the coyote's failed attempts.

Your child will learn basic physics while guffawing over Wile E. Coyote's poorly planned efforts to get ahold of Road Runner. Wile E. uses levers, pulleys, screws, and wheels and axles to build clever traps, but each simple machine fails. And why are his experiments with forces and motion as unsuccessful as his experiments using speed and velocity? Will gravity work for him or against him as he tries out various flying contraptions? Wile E. Coyote, Physical Science Genius is a lighthearted introduction

to the essential principles that govern physical science in our daily lives.

Scheduling

With just over 100 pages in all, plan on just 2 to 3 a week to finish in a year—if your child can stand to wait that long!

PIXIO 200

BASIC COMPLETE **ELITE**

Now your child can create dozens of pixel-style models with Pixio 200. This colorful magnetic construction set allows children to create objects, characters, and structures using super-tiny, about the size of a pea, ABS plastic cubes that connect on all sides.

Inside each of the cubes are six powerful magnets that allow models to be easily assembled and disassembled. The Neodymium magnets are powerful enough to stay intact, but not so strong that taking models apart is difficult.

Each Pixio 200 set includes a unique code to use for exclusive content on the Pixio free, downloadable app where there are countless interactive, 3-D design ideas to explore.

The magnets may seem to make building slow because you have to line up the polarity of each block, but once your child gets the hang of adding only one block at a time so the magnets can rotate and connect, building is a snap. Pixio 200I will help your child develop fine motor skills, spatial reasoning, creativity, and problem-solving.

Scheduling

Unlimited. We suggest completing at least two models a week - one from the app and one that's their own design. This cultivates both convergent and divergent thinking, as we suggest in our article on page 82.

STEM OR STEAM?

STEM, an acronym for Science, Technology, Engineering, and Mathematics, has recently been joined by Art to form STEAM. Is it really that important? Yes! Art is used to plan the layout of a tower, the design of a prosthetic hand, and the colors of the latest app. In fact, as long as your project is inquiry-based and you have the opportunity to think critically, creatively, and innovatively, then you are looking at a STEAM curriculum. Because the transition of terminology from STEM to STEAM is still tentative, we are using STEM for clarity's sake and listing art here separately in this handbook. But don't let that fool you into overlooking art this year. It really is a vital skill!

STEP-BY-STEP DRAWING BOOK

~~BASIC~~ **COMPLETE ~ ELITE**

Complete beginners can discover how to draw lots of different things, from dogs to dragons and cats to castles, in this delightful write-in book. Each colorful double-page has step-by-step drawing instructions, plenty of space to practice, and occasional ideas for adding embellishment or pizzazz to the drawings.

Step-By-Step Drawing Book instructions are easy to follow, so children of all ages can effortlessly master the simple drawing skills required to depict a range of animals and objects.

If your child isn't yet sold on the beauty of art, this book may provide him the skill he needs to enjoy it. It may also be helpful to ponder why his dream profession would be even better with art skills. For instance, firefighters need to be able to draw their rescue plans on the marker board during training. Doctors often draw out the medical ailments afflicting their patients to explain why they are recommending a specific treatment plan. And we all know that parents and teachers alike benefit from some drawing skills! If your schedule allows, spend some time drawing with your child - it's a beautiful time for connection, and also models that you really do think this is a worthy skill!

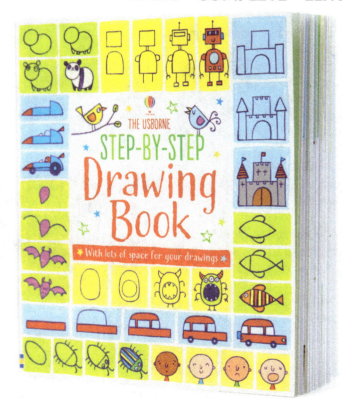

Scheduling
Complete one to two double-page spreads per week.

ME: A COMPENDIUM

~~BASIC ~~ **COMPLETE ~ ELITE**

We get it, you're busy. And all the precious memories from your child's life are fading quickly. We don't have a solution that will solve all of that brain drain, but we do have one that will allow you to preserve a tiny slice, and better still, allows your child to be part of the solution.

Me: A Compendium is a humorously illustrated, library-worthy hardback book that your child fills with drawings and words that reveal his likes and dislikes, and what exactly makes him tick. In this lighthearted celebration of your child, he will be asked to record his favorite joke, pick a name for his band, disclose his best hiding place, and reveal how he thinks he will look at 50.

Some parts of Me: A Compendium need written-out answers and other parts need pictures drawn–very doable for your second-grader. And don't forget to look under the dustcover for additional hidden gems.

Inventive, hilarious, and joyously colorful, Me: A Compendium will become a keepsake glimpse of your child's unique personality.

Still wondering why this would be considered an educational priority? Several years ago the top buzzword for business was "creative." A few years later, the hot topic in education became creativity. This trickle-down development should spur educators, especially those of us teaching at home, to look beyond easy "read-and-regurgitate" education that dulls the mind. Instead, we should lead a lifestyle that not only encourages imaginative efforts, but that also passionately carves out time for those pursuits every day.

Scheduling

We've chosen to count these pages by spreads, to make sure your child isn't frustrated by having to walk away mid-project. Warm up the creative side of your child by completing one to two spreads a week. (Don't forget to do the ones on the cover and over-wrap, too!)

64   www.timberdoodle.com • ©2019

NATURAL WORLD WORKSHOP
~~BASIC~~ COMPLETE ~ ELITE

Using highly pigmented yet easy to work with gouache paint, Natural World Workshop is a step above the traditional children's paint-by-numbers sets. Each of the four large prints is already partly illustrated, the more difficult parts of each scene already colored in. Following the full-color picture instruction book, young artists are clearly shown how to complete these original pictures of nature. By applying the bright, opaque paints to the correct numbers, your child will create beautiful pictures of animals, birds and sea creatures all in their natural habitat. Natural World Workshop makes an enjoyable activity for children who love art and nature! Natural World Workshop comes with four code printed boards, eight colorful opaque paints and a brush to complete the masterpieces.

Scheduling
With four lovely paintings to complete, we suggest working on one a month, ideally spending about 20 minutes a week on it.

Bring exotic fish to life in this fun variation on the classic paint-by-numbers art kit. Just peel, sprinkle, and enjoy. Fish Rainbows includes four pre-printed images of beautiful fish for your child to complete, all necessary supplies, and a detailed wordless instruction booklet.

Ingeniously designed to conserve sand, the sturdy Fish Rainbows box has a small hole in one corner, allowing you to shake in leftover sand and pour it back into the sand containers.

The sand pots are a bit tough to open, so your young artist will need your help removing the lids.

Scheduling

We suggest working on one a month, ideally spending about 20 minutes a week on it. You can choose whether to alternate months with Natural World Workshop, or complete one kit in its entirety before beginning the next.

LET THEM WIGGLE!

When one of our children was a preschooler, we received the best advice a parent of a kinesthetic child could receive: Let her wiggle. And wiggle she did. I don't think she sat for schoolwork for many years. But she learned! The negative? Pirouettes and somersaults can be a huge distraction to a child's siblings.

A workable compromise is a handheld fidget like Mad Mattr that lets your child work his muscles and keep his brain active without him whirling around the room!

The other learning tool in this section is a test prep guide that will help you and your child go into any mandatory testing with a big boost in confidence.

MAD MATTR

~~BASIC~~ **COMPLETE ~ ELITE**

A Swedish phenomenon that has swept throughout Europe like wildfire is now available in the US! Mad Mattr, an amazingly moldable, stretchable, dough-like compound, can be shaped into countless brilliantly colored creations. Silky to the touch, Mad Mattr never dries out – ever.

Wheat-, gluten-, casein-, and odor-free, Mad Mattr is firm to the touch, but will quickly loosen to be soft, airy, and malleable. Pressed against a textured surface, Mad Mattr makes a stunningly accurate imprint. Or pull it apart gently and it will stream into a puddle on your table.

Unleash your child's creative side without destroying your home with Mad Mattr. Virtually mess-free, it doesn't stain and won't stick to your carpet, furniture, clothes, or books. And the bits and pieces that materialize on your work surface are easily gathered, sticking to one another and not to the table.

In fact, it is for that very reason that we've included Mad Mattr as a learning tool this year. It packs all the benefits of Thinking Putty as a fidget, but without the mess or potential for household damage!

Scheduling

There really are unlimited ways to use this tool. Its primary purpose is that of a fidget, perfect for your child to play with while he watches his math lessons, or at other times when his mind is more engaged than his hands. Are you looking for specific things to do with Mad Mattr? Check out pages 98-102 for 36 different ideas to liven up your Mad Mattr time each week. (Some second-graders will have outgrown these ideas, while others will relish them. Try them with your child and see what he thinks!)

SPECTRUM TEST PRACTICE

~~BASIC~~ COMPLETE ~ ELITE

At the end of the year, use Spectrum Test Practice to prepare your child for annual testing (if your state requires it) and to review what he has learned. Even if your state doesn't require testing, consider completing the book anyway, since test-taking skills are vital across all areas of life. Since online resources include language arts and math practice tests for individual state alignments, don't forget to check those out before the "real" test.

Scheduling

Our family has always preferred to spend the week or two before our state-mandated annual testing working through this book. Keep it low key, and let the change of pace be an enjoyable experience for your child. If you run into a concept he doesn't know, stop and explain it to him; that is why you are doing the prep now!

FROM OUR FAMILY TO YOURS

In 1986, we were a family of five. I was the oldest of three toddler girls with a mom who absolutely excelled at educating us at home. Of course, this was during "The Dark Ages" of homeschooling, and online searching was still a thing of the future. Our mom, Deb, was (and is) a voracious reader, though, and an avid researcher. We girls were thriving academically and, naturally, other moms were interested in using the same curricula Deb had found.

So, in 1986 she and Dan, our dad, repurposed the business license originally intended for their world-class Golden Retriever breeding operation (which had come to naught) and she launched Timberdoodle, a homeschool supply company. A catalog was born, and growth came fast. We shipped from our laundry room, the grandparents' basement, and finally, warehouses and an office. Two more children were added, and all of us grew up working in the business from an early age.

Now, decades later, Timberdoodle is still renowned for out-of-the-box learning and crazy-smart finds. Mom's engineering background has heavily influenced our STEM selections, and her no-nonsense, independent approach has made these kits the award-winning choice that they are today.

All five of us are grown now, and most still work at Timberdoodle in key roles. Abel and his wife are homeschooling their young ones, while my sisters and I have opened our lives to fostering children. The kits we sell are the same ones we use in our own homes, and we hope you enjoy them as much as we do.

In the following articles, you'll hear from Deb and others about some of the nitty-gritty questions we often field. Do you have a question not answered here? Don't forget that you are invited to contact us at any time; we'd love to help!

Joy (for all of us)

MY SECOND-GRADER CAN'T LISTEN!

HOW TO TEACH AUDITORY PROCESSING WITHOUT LOSING YOUR MIND

Timberdoodle kits are renowned for hands-on components, which means that many of you switched to Timberdoodle specifically to help your kinesthetic learner. Yay! It's perfect!

But then you find a problem. Your science and history courses this year rely on a lot of listening unless your student is reading far above his grade level. Some students will hang on every word, while for others listening for an entire chapter will be a huge challenge.

So now what? Is this a battle worth fighting? We would argue that it definitely is! As your student gets older, he will find more and more frequently that he needs to be able to take in and utilize information he receives only through his ears. (Side note: Have you ever considered that it is nearly impossible to teach history without using words? After all, there are many horrific historical moments that you want to be able to discuss, not reenact!)

If you find that your student struggles to stay focused, there are a few things to keep in mind.

First, he's not alone. Every second-grade classroom is filled with bubbly little kids whose attention splits at a moment's notice. Science and history are introductory materials at this grade level, and they will all be revisited in more depth at a later time. So if you feel like there is information that they aren't retaining, you're probably right, but you shouldn't find that discouraging!

Also, these courses were written for a range of grades. Some of the material is geared for the older siblings in the group, though you may be surprised by how much of that your second-grader can actually grasp with the proper training!

Now, on a practical note, getting his hands busy might help:

- You could get out the activity pages/notebooking pages first, so that he can color while you read.
- Maybe he'd prefer to grab his LEGO® bricks and build while he listens.
- Break out the Mad Mattr–it's in your kit particularly for such a time as this!

Now that he's set up, start reading. You want to read up until just before his attention wanders. If he's a typical second-grader, a page or two may be the perfect amount to start with!

Read a portion, and then ask him what happened/what the point was/if he thought X was actually going to work... If he can answer, set the book aside and move to whatever is his "fun part" of school. (You'll come back to the book portion by portion throughout the day.) If he struggles, read the portion again and give him another try at answering. As time goes by, you'll be able to read larger and larger portions at once.

The beauty of this approach is that you are actively working to build his auditory processing, an essential learning skill.

If this continues to be an issue, it is never a bad idea to loop your pediatrician into the conversation. You may find that there is a physical component (such as hearing impairment) that is an underlying issues and really should be addressed.

Some kids will always be wiggly and that is just fine. Your goal is to equip your wiggler to learn in all the ways he can, and homeschooling is ideal for that!

WHY EMPHASIZE INDEPENDENT LEARNING?

THE TOP SEVEN REASONS THIS IS SUCH A BIG DEAL AT TIMBERDOODLE

1. Avoid Burn Out

One-on-one teaching is critical to the success of any student, and homeschoolers are no exception to that. However, we have seen parents who become helicopter educators, micromanaging every detail of their students' education. Is it any wonder that these parents burn out? Independent learning tools provide a natural transition from the one-on-one of early childhood to a less parent-intense educational approach.

2. Cultivate Responsible Learners

There is a lot of (dare we say it?) fun in teaching. But it is better for your students if they master how to learn on their own. After all, when they are adults, you'll want them to have the ability to pick up any skill they want and learn it as needed. Structuring their education to be more and more self-taught helps them to become responsible self-learners.

3. Special Needs, Illness, and Newborns

Not all parents have the same amount of teaching time. Whether they are doing therapy for a child with autism, dealing with their own chronic illness, managing visits for a foster child, or are blessed with a newborn, there are seasons when homeschooling needs to be more independent simply for the teacher's sanity!

4. You Don't Have to Love Teaching

As much as no one wants to mention this, we all know parents who really struggle to teach. They love their kids and feel strongly about homeschooling, but when it actually comes down to teaching they are easily overwhelmed and intimidated. If it is an area they are not gifted/trained in, then of course teaching is scary. Independent learning tools can help get them comfortable in their role, but even if they never love teaching they can still reap the benefits of giving their children a superior education at home.

5. Timberdoodle's Purpose: We Are Here to Make Giving Your Children a Superior Education at Home Enjoyable

Here at Timberdoodle, amid the catalogs, sales, blog posts, videos, Facebook giveaways, etc., we have one primary goal. That goal is to make it possible for parents to enjoy giving their children a superior education at home. We aren't here to sell you stuff (though we wouldn't exist if you didn't shop!), which is why we have been known to send you to our "competitors" when their product would work better for you. We really just want you to be a happy homeschool family. When that happens, we feel successful! Independent learning is one tool in your toolbox. It is a valuable tool, so use it where it works best for you.

6. Not Either/Or

You don't have to pick between independent and group learning across the board. Take The Fallacy Detective, for instance. It is designed for a student to pick up and read independently. Instead, our family did it as a read-aloud and took turns answering the questions. The result? Not only did we have a blast, but we were also all on the same page regarding logical fallacies. Bumper stickers and ads we came across in daily life were fodder for vigorous discussions about the underlying fallacies in ways that would never

have happened if we each studied it alone. So even if you're striving to teach independent learning, don't hesitate to do some things together!

7. Our Family

The rule of thumb in our house was that as soon as a child could read, he or she was responsible for his or her own education. We each had an annual conference with Mom to set learning goals for the year, then were given the books for the year, often including the teacher's manuals. Mom gave us each a weekly checklist to complete before Friday Family Night. If we needed help, we were to ask for it. Otherwise, the responsibility was ours. This freed us up to do the truly important things (devotions, service, Timberdoodle work, babysitting, elder care, church projects, hospitality, farming...) as a family.

10 REASONS TO STOP SCHOOL WORK AND GO BUILD SOMETHING!

Would you like to supplement your curriculum with a program that simultaneously improves your child's visual perception, fine motor skills, patience, problem solving, spatial perception, creativity, ability to follow directions, pre-reading skills, grasp of physics concepts, and engineering ability? Better yet, what if your child would actually enjoy this curriculum and choose to do it whenever he could? No, this isn't some mythical homeschool product guaranteed to solve all your problems for a large fee—we are talking about the LEGO® bricks already strewn throughout your house, the blocks in our preschool curriculum, and the Bioloid robot kit designed for teens.

Construction kits just might be the most underrated type of curriculum ever. It's not just us; research concludes that children learn a lot by designing and building things. Based on our own engineering background/bias, we believe that construction is one of the most valuable educational processes available and that both learning to build and learning by what has been built should be a part of every family's curriculum. Here are our top 10 skills your child will learn with his construction kit:

1. Visual Perception
It may be obvious that it takes visual perception to find the right pieces and place them well, but consider that whether your child is reading, finishing a puzzle, or doing open-heart surgery, a proficiency in visual perception is mandatory!

2. Fine Motor Skills
Boys especially seem to struggle with fine motor skills, particularly when it comes to writing and drawing. Amazingly

enough, though, they are often the most passionate about building—the natural remedy! The more they fine-tune their dexterity, the easier "school time" becomes for both of you!

3. Patience

Do you know anyone who couldn't stand to be a little more patient? Construction takes time. Slowing down, reading the directions, doing it over when a piece has been placed wrong or a sibling knocks over your creation… these are all valuable character-building experiences!

4. Problem Solving

Some children simply lack the ability to troubleshoot a situation and figure out the next step. Construction sets provide a structured opportunity to figure out what went wrong and fix it, if you're following the directions. If you are designing your own models, you'll have even more opportunities to problem solve!

5. Spatial Perception

Probably the clearest picture of how important it is to be able to mentally convert 2-D images into 3-D objects is that of a surgeon. Knowing where the spleen is on a 2-D textbook page isn't nearly the same thing as being able to reach into an incision and find the damaged spleen!

6. Creativity

Not every creative person has artistic ability. But construction can open the doors of creativity like no other tool. What if I move this gear over here? Could I build that bridge with only blue pieces?

7. Following Directions

Some children are natural rule followers and need to be encouraged to be creative. Others need to constrain themselves to follow directions, at least on occasion! If your child falls into that camp, construction kits are a natural way to encourage him in this skill, with the added benefit of a finished result he can show off!

8. Pre-Reading Skills

Did you know that a child who cannot duplicate a pattern will be a poor candidate for reading and writing? Not only that, but the use of pattern duplication is a proven approach to helping prepare children to understand abstract math concepts and higher-order thinking. But if you have a scholar who rolls his eyes at working with pattern blocks and sighs deeply when asked to replicate a design with traditional four-sided blocks, you need construction kits!

9. Grasp of Physics

Friction, force, mass, and energy are all basic physics concepts much more easily explained and grasped with a set of blocks and a ball than simply by studying a dry textbook definition!

10. Engineering Ability

Many "born engineers" are not drawn to textbooks. But set a construction kit in front of them and watch them explore pulleys, levers, wheels, and gears. They'll soon go from exploration to innovation, and you'll be amazed at their inventions!

WHAT IF THIS IS TOO HARD?

9 STEPS TO TAKE IF YOU'RE FEELING OVERWHELMED

Everyone has felt overwhelmed at some point in his or her education. Whether it's a groan from you as you pull a giant textbook out of the box or the despair from your child when he's read the directions five times and the robot STILL isn't operating as he wants it to, you will almost certainly hit a moment this year when you realize that an aspect of homeschooling is harder than you anticipated.

So, what do you do now?

1. Take a Breath
Just knowing that everyone faces this should help you relax a bit. This feeling will not last - you'll get through this!

2. Jump In!
Why are you stressed right now? Are you stressed because "it" is so intimidating that you haven't been quite ready to tackle it? If that's the case, the simplest solution is to jump in and get started. Could you read the first page together before lunch? What if you have your student find all of the pieces for step one today? Sometimes it's better to muddle through a lesson together than to wait until you're ready to teach it perfectly.

3. Step Back
Perhaps you're too close right now. If you're mid-project with incredible effort and totally frustrated by how it's going, try the opposite approach. Close the book for 30 minutes (set a timer!) and go grab lunch, hit the playground, or swap to a more hands-on project. When the timer rings, you and your student will be ready to try again with clearer heads.

4. Time This
Timers are an invaluable learning tool. If you're being distracted, try setting a 10- or 20-minute timer during which you'll do only ___. Or tell yourself you definitely need to tackle That Dreaded Subject, but only for 30 minutes a day, in two 15-minute chunks. When the timer rings, close the text and move to the next thing. Dividing your day into blocks of time can make a remarkable difference in your efficiency level.

5. Level Down
Did your student take the math pre-test before jumping in this year? Perhaps he is just in the wrong level! If moving to an easier level kind of freaks you out, it may help to remember that you and your student are not defined by his skill set in any field, and faking his way through by blood, sweat, and tears does not help his future self. Taking the time to back up and fill in the gaps, though, that will benefit him forever!

6. Simplify
If you are trying to do every possible activity in every course, it's no wonder you're exhausted. By the time your student is in high school, he will need to complete 75% or more of the work in each course to get full credits. We're not advocates of doing the work in name only, but it's okay to watch some experiments online rather than completing each one in the

dining room. It's also appropriate to only do every other math problem in a section if your child is bored to tears with yet another page of addition. Doesn't that feel better?

7. Make Accommodations

What exactly is stressing your student (or you!) out right now? Is it the pen-to-paper writing component? Why not let him use the computer and type his work instead? Or perhaps he can dictate to you while you write for him. Make sure you're doing whatever you can to engage his best learning style. Encourage Mr. Auditory Learner to read aloud if necessary. Or break out all of the favorite fidgets and let Miss Kinesthetic work at a standing desk.

8. Get Help

Ask another teacher/parent to take some time working through the issue with you. You may be surprised by how much clarity you gain with a fresh set of eyes. (Our Facebook groups can be great for this!)

9. Get Professional Help

Check the publisher's website, the book's teacher page, or the kit's manual for contact information. Most of the

authors and manufacturers we work with are fantastic about helping and coaching those who get stuck. Not getting the help you need from them? Contact mail@Timberdoodle.com or call us at 800-478-0672 and we'll work with them to get that answer for you.

9 TIPS FOR HOMESCHOOLING GIFTED CHILDREN

1. Disdain Busy Work
Your child wants to learn, so don't slow him down! If he has mastered multiplication, why are you still spending an hour a day reviewing it? Yes, he does need some review, but we've seen way too many families focus on completing every problem rather than mastering the material. One way to test this is to have him try doing only every other review problem and see how he does. If he can prove he's mastered it, he doesn't need to be spending quite as much time on it.

2. Go Deep
Allow breathing room in your schedule so you have time to investigate earth's gravitational pull or the advantages/disadvantages of hair sheep vs. wooly sheep. Remember that your child is asking to learn, so why pull him away from the subject that's fascinating him? After all, we all know that material we're interested in sticks with us so much better than things we learn only because we must.

3. Go Fast
If your child wants to take three science courses this year or race through two math levels, then why not let him? Homeschoolers can absolutely rock this, because there are no peers holding them to a "traditional" pace!

4. Encourage Completion
Sometimes it seems there is a touch of ADD in every genius. Give your child as much flexibility as you possibly can, but also keep in mind that you'll be doing him a disservice if he never has to tackle something he doesn't feel like working on at the moment. Sometimes he may even be surprised to realize that the very subject he dreaded is the springboard for a whole new area of investigation!

5. Give Space & Opportunities
If you can keep mandatory studies to a minimum, you'll give your child more opportunities to accelerate his learning in the areas he's gifted at. Common sense, perhaps, but also worth deliberately thinking through as you plan out your school year.

6. Work on Weak Areas Carefully

While you definitely want to work with him to help him overcome areas he's just not as strong in, you also want to be careful that a weakness in one area doesn't impede his progress in other ways. For instance, a child may struggle with writing simply because his brain works much faster than his hands. While we encourage such a family to work on handwriting skills, we also suggest that they try teaching their child to type and allow him to complete writing assignments on the computer. This lets him continue to build his writing skills instead of holding him back because of his lack of handwriting speed.

7. Emphasize Humility & Service

We have met way too many children who are obnoxiously convinced that they are geniuses and that everyone needs to be in awe of their abilities. Your child will be much healthier (and happier!) if he realizes these four things:

- His identity is NEVER found in his brainpower.

- Even as gifted as he is, there are still things that others do better than he does.

- He is much more than his brain. (Should he lose his "edge," he won't lose his worth!)

- His gifts are not for himself alone but for serving God and His people.

Of course, the goal is never to insult or degrade him, but to give him a framework from which he can truly thrive and be free to learn. With a proper perspective, he'll be able to enjoy learning without the burden of constantly assessing his genius and worrying what people will think of him. Don't weigh him down by constantly telling him how big his brain is, either. Encourage his learning, but don't forget to cultivate his character at all costs. In 10 years, his response to rebuke will be much more telling than his test score this year, so don't put an inordinate stress on intellectual pursuits.

8. Talk, a LOT!

Talk about what he's interested in. Talk about the theories he came up with today. Talk about his daydreams. Talk about what he wants to study up on. Talk about why he may actually need to master that most-dreadful-of-subjects, whatever that may be to him... Not only will you be able to impart your years of wisdom to him, but you'll also know well the subjects he's interested in and be able to tie those in to his other studies, the places you're visiting next week, or that interesting article you read yesterday.

9. Relax!

Your child is a wonderful gift; don't feel that every moment must be spent maximizing his potential. As a side benefit, just relaxing about his genius may in fact increase it. Our own family found that some of our best test scores came after a year off of most formal schooling! Not what we would have planned, but a very valuable insight. Living life=learning, so maximize that!

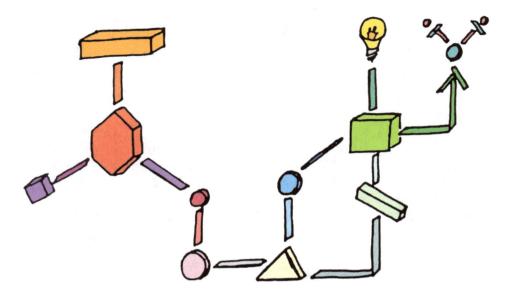

CONVERGENT & DIVERGENT THINKING

Have you considered the necessity of incorporating both convergent and divergent thinking into your learning time? Experts recognize these as the two major types of brain challenges we all encounter.

Does that just sound like a whole bunch of big words? No worries, let's break it down. Your child needs to be able to find the right answer when needed (math, medicine dosage) and also needs to be able to come up with a creative, unscripted answer when the situation warrants (art, architecture...).

A child who can only find the "right" answer will be a rigid thinker who can't problem-solve well or think outside the box.

A child who only thinks creatively will not be able to follow procedures or do anything that involves math.

What Is Convergent Thinking?

To go more in-depth, convergent thinking generally involves finding a single best answer and is important in the study of math and science. Convergent thinking is the backbone of the majority of curricula and is crucial for future engineers, doctors, and even parents. Much of daily life is a series of determining right and wrong answers, and standardized tests favor the convergent thinker. But when we pursue only convergent-rich curricula we miss the equally vital arena of divergent thinking.

Is Divergent Thinking Different?

Yes! Divergent thinking encourages your child's mind to explore many possible solutions, maybe even ideas that aren't necessarily apparent at first. It is in use when he discovers that there is more than one way to build a bridge with blocks, to animate a movie, or even simply to complete a doodle. Radically different from read-and-regurgitate

www.timberdoodle.com • ©2019

textbooks, divergent activities are not only intellectually stimulating, but kids love them, too.

Make a Conscious Effort to Include Both in Your Curriculum

Admittedly, because most textbooks and even puzzles are designed for convergent thinking, you will need to make a conscious effort to expose your children to multiple opportunities for divergent thinking. It is imperative because both divergent and convergent thinking are necessary for critical thinking to be effective.

Why Doctors Need Both Skills

As an example, let's look at a medical doctor. A physician needs to be extraordinarily skilled at convergent thinking to dose medications correctly, diagnose life-threatening

emergencies, and follow safety procedures to avoid infection. However, the first person to wash their hands before surgery, or to find a treatment for Ebola, used divergent thinking. Some of the best doctors today are those who employ powerful convergent skills to accurately diagnose, paired with curiosity and divergent thinking to find the most effective or previously undiscovered treatment plans.

Convergent in Second Grade?

From reading to math, the backbone of your curriculum this year is convergent. This makes sense, because so much of learning at this level is simply marveling at facts. Sometimes there really is a right answer!

Is Divergent in Second Grade?

Yes! These tools all include strong divergent aspects to help your child become a well-rounded thinker:

- **Pixio 200**
- **Me: A Compendium**
- **My First Story Writing Book**
- **Mad Mattr**

Beyond that, many other items in this kit can provide opportunities for both convergent and divergent thinking. For instance, as he recreates exact models from Engino Inventor, he's working on convergent skills. But when he revises a model to add a feature or builds a model from his imagination, that's capitalizing on divergent learning.

WHY ISN'T THERE A BIBLE COURSE?

OUR FAVORITE BIBLE TOOLS, 4 WAYS WE'VE DONE DEVOTIONS, AND MORE

From the time our children could sit in our laps, family devotion was a mainstay in our home, so teaching Bible to our children was paramount. But for too many families the sum total of Bible instruction for their children is Bible workbooks that are little more than read-and-regurgitate exercises, and that alarms me. Yes, we do want children to know the facts of the Bible – who killed a giant with a small stone, who was thrown into a lion's den, and who changed water into wine–and resources such as The Action Bible do a splendid job of teaching those facts. But my experience has been that children need massive amounts of intimate daily input to fully grasp the glory of the gospel, and there is no easier way than through a daily family devotion.

Then What About Requiring Each Child to Read Their Bibles Every Day?

That is certainly the trajectory we all want for our children, but how is that working for you personally? Have you ever had times where you 'read' your daily chapter(s) while thinking about dinner, the toddler meltdown, or updating your shopping list? Your children have the same struggles.

How Is a Daily Devotional Different?

With a daily devotional, the Bible reading can be explored in a much more personal manner. You know your children better than any publisher, and if the prescribed questions are not relevant to the sins and follies of your child, you can adapt and even drill down further. You can also use that time to point out how the Word is living and active in your own life with personal anecdotes that pertain to the topic at hand.

Then Can't You Include Devotional Materials with Each Grade Level?

No, for the simple reason that many of our favorite devotional materials, in particular Long Story Short and Old Story New, are usable for multiple ages and multiple years. And because God's work in each family is unique, we are much more comfortable exposing you to what we consider the best all-around resources and letting you cherry pick the most appropriate for your use and your situation.

What Does the Ideal Devotional Look Like?

We are ardent proponents of reading the Bible every day. For the little ones there is The Big Picture Story Bible, slightly older ones will enjoy The Jesus Storybook Bible, and then they should be ready for Long Story Short and Old Story New. But don't stop there, add in great theological books that you have enjoyed. When our children were little we read books by John Piper, Ravi Zacharias, R.C. Sproul, Randy Alcorn, and Martyn Lloyd-Jones. We read them slowly, sometimes just a page or two a day, pausing often to discuss the concepts and how they related to our lives, the lives of their friends, and the world at large. Every devotional time ended with a chapter out of a true-to-life story, both Christian and secular, where opportunities again presented themselves to discuss motivations, temptations, and how God's Word pertains to this situation.

Do You Have Specific Recommendations for Second Grade?

We are big fans of:
Everyone a Child Should Know
Everything a Child Should Know About God
Everything a Child Should Know About Prayer
The Jesus Storybook Bible
The Biggest Story
Long Story Short
Old Story New

Thoughts to Make Your Heart Sing
Indescribable
The Ology: Ancient Truths Ever New...
The Action Bible
Cat & Dog Theology...
 And that's just the highlights! To see
our most current favorites just pop by
the website. (Also, keep in mind that
if you have reward points on file, this
could be a wonderful way to use them.)

What Do Your Family Devotions Really Look Like?

As you can imagine, this shifts
dramatically over time. Let me give you
four different snap shots from recent
years:

2016: Herding Cats

As a foster family with little ones 1-4 years old, devotion time
has radically changed from previous years when we were a
family of grown-ups!

Our morning devotion routine starts with gathering the
family and getting the little ones seated quietly on the couch.
Honestly, this is probably the most difficult part! Some
mornings are (finally!) almost effortless, but some mornings
way more time is spent on obedience than on devotions. Not
to worry, this is both normal and extraordinarily valuable for
the children. In fact, the toddlers probably benefit more from
that training than from the actual contents of devotion time.

Once everyone is seated, we briefly review yesterday's
lesson and read a new page from Everything a Child Should
Know About God. We're loving this book for our current
little ones as it covers the basics in a paragraph or two every
day–perfect for tiny attention spans!

We then do our memory verse of the week. Right now we're
using Foundation Fighter Verses to help us select meaningful
texts, and we're setting every verse to ASL sign. We're all
learning and signing it together, keeping everyone engaged.

Finally, we end with a simple song, again with sign language.
On occasion we've found a YouTube video showing other
kids singing and signing, and that's always a bonus. But we've
found that just learning it together works well also, and that
gives us a much broader selection of songs to pick from.

All told, this is probably a 5- to 10-minute process. While

more could be added (I'm eager to add more catechism components as one of our kids loves those), we're very excited to see our little ones learning the story line and theology of the Bible in a way that they enjoy.

In the evening we watch another chapter from The Jesus Storybook Bible DVDs together just before tucking our little ones in for the night. Much of it goes over their heads, but it is a wonderful way to end the day for all of us.

2017: Including Aspects from Church
Our little ones are now ages 2.5 to almost 5, and our morning devotions have shifted slightly.

Our main lesson now comes from The Beginner's Gospel Story Bible. It is as vibrant and interesting as our little ones are, and it does a wonderful job of presenting the gospel as seen throughout the Bible.

Our church uses The Gospel Project, so we end our morning

devotions with this week's Big Picture Q & A, memory verse, and song. The familiarity of hearing the exact same thing at church on Sunday is really good for our children, and it's good for us, too!

This is still probably a 5 to 10 minute process. While more could be added, we're very

excited to see our little ones learning the story line and theology of the Bible in a way that they enjoy.

We've already switched our evening devotions to an advent theme since we have high ambitions for their Christmas memory work. Each child is invited to hold a (battery operated!) candle and clutch a stuffed goat (from "the shepherd's flock") while we all sing a handful of Christmas carols and then recite the Christmas story from Luke 2. It is a wonderful way to end the day for all of us!

2018: Advent
We're forgoing a formal morning routine now, and instead whoever is working with the kids on any particular morning gets some Bible time in with them, in whatever format works best for them (rereading a Bible book, modifying a Sunday school curriculum, etc...)

Our oldest is also doing Bible time during her daily school time with Aunt Pearl, who has a routine adapted from Exploring the Bible where she reads portions of the Scripture as the five-year-old does her STEM work or other hands-only work. They then highlight what they've read to mark their progress. This child struggles with auditory processing so Pearl is always working to fine-tune the method and make it work for her.

At night, though, we all gather and light the Advent candles. (We chose the Advent Wreath with a new candle every day.) We then sing an increasing number of Christmas carols, adding a new one every week, and recite a chunk of Luke 2 together. We end with a small chocolate for all participants.

This is a change of pace from our regular routine, and it

allows us all to absorb more of the wonders of the season together.

2019: Gratitude and Chaos

Our five little ones now range from babies to a five-year-old, and we're finding that we need to be punctual in our routine or the chaos ensues quickly.

The morning and school routines remain unchanged for now, and evening is when the formal Bible time happens.

After everyone is in his or her jammies and ready for bed we sing a hymn of the week together. No one is reading yet, so we choose hymns with repetition and themes that will be relevant. (We're by no means a hymns-only family, but there is a richness there that we so want our little ones to taste.)

We then read a chapter from The Beginner's Gospel Story Bible together, usually while the reader and the little ones sprawl all over the floor. We've done this book before, but it's been long enough that the kids are enjoying the repetition and getting more out of it this time through.

Once that is done, the "big kids" (ages 3-5) grab their gratitude journals and adult buddies, and together we write and draw something they are grateful for about the day. (The child dictates, we scribe and illustrate.) This is a concept we're still working to cement in their minds, but it is so valuable to both help their brains retain memories and to help them see every good gift as coming from God.

The kids reconvene in the living room a few minutes later for a chapter from a just-for-fun bedtime story.

So What's Your Plan?

This year has the potential for rich and vibrant growth in your child's life. Don't put off making any decisions or you'll end the year right where you started. We'd encourage you to jump in and try something. Not working well? Tweak it! Find the best time of day, content, and format for your family right now, and don't be afraid to make changes as needed.

HELP! MY BOOK SAYS "COMMON CORE"!

THE TRUTH ABOUT WHETHER YOUR TIMBERDOODLE CURRICULUM KIT IS ALIGNED WITH COMMON CORE

There's been a lot of buzz, discussion, and anxiety in the homeschool community for the last nine years about the Common Core State Standards. Many of you have asked us what our stance is on the standards and whether our curriculum is designed to comply with them.

What Is the Common Core?

According to the CCSS website, "The Common Core State Standards Initiative is a state-led effort that established a single set of clear educational standards for kindergarten through 12th grade in English language arts and mathematics that states voluntarily adopt."

But Isn't That a Good Idea?

Growing up as an Air Force "brat," Deb, Timberdoodle's founder, attended many different schools throughout her educational career. She can tell you just how much easier it would have been for her if all of the schools covered the same materials in the same order. Then, she could transfer effortlessly between them instead of missing critical information because the new school had already covered something her old school hadn't addressed yet. So, yes, the concept may be brilliant, but there are some very valid concerns.

Why Homeschoolers Are Concerned

There is some real concern in the homeschooling community about what the Common Core Standards Initiative will mean to our families. In an early article posted by the Homeschool Legal Defense Association, HSLDA Director of Federal Relations William Estrada wrote, "The CCSS specifically do not apply to private or homeschools... However, HSLDA has serious concerns with the rush to adopt the CCSS. HSLDA has fought national education standards for the past two decades. Why? National standards lead to national curriculum and national tests, and subsequent pressure on homeschool students to be taught from the same curricula."

Declining Quality?

Some in the homeschooling community have also expressed concern that as curriculum publishers endeavor to align with the CCSS, the educational quality in those texts will actually decrease rather than improve, while some are disenchanted with the atypical teaching methods employed by the CCSS, among other concerns.

What We Are Doing

At Timberdoodle, our approach is simple. We are ignoring the CCSS and continuing to search out crazy-smart curricula, exactly what we've been doing for the past 30+ years. Our specialty has always been hand-picking the best products in every subject area and offering the families who trust us the same products we have used or would happily use ourselves. And we have no plans to change the way we carefully review every resource we sell.

Some Products Do Say Common Core

Some of the items in this kit do, in fact, align with the CCSS. Not because we've sought that out, but because the quality resources we've chosen for our curriculum are already up to that standard or beyond. It is no surprise to us that the excellent tools we are excited about are also good enough to exceed the qualifications for the CCSS.

This Has Never Changed and Will Not Change Now

At Timberdoodle, we work with trusted publishers and products we review carefully, not just in math and language arts but in all subject areas, so that we feel confident we are providing some of the best resources available for your children. Every time an item we've loved is revised (or stamped Common Core), we make sure that it has not been watered down or made confusing. Our goal is to exceed educational requirements, not by aligning our curriculum with any government standard, but by continuing to find products that work well and meet the high standards we hold for our families and yours.

512 BOOK SUGGESTIONS/IDEAS

So you love the idea of the reading challenge, but you'd like a boost to get you started? You've come to the right place!

Customize This!

You'll find a few ideas here for each challenge, but don't forget that you're not bound to our list. There are literally hundreds more options that may be even better for your family. Use these pages as starter ideas and not as your final list.

Will I See the Same Books Over and Over?

No, not on this list! However, you can expect to see some of these books appear on the lists for more than one grade (so 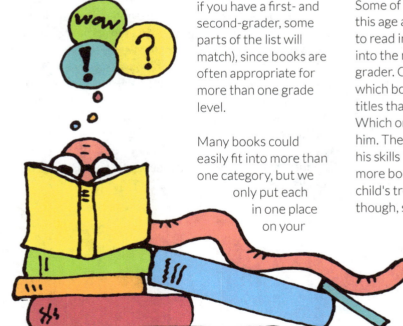 if you have a first- and second-grader, some parts of the list will match), since books are often appropriate for more than one grade level.

Many books could easily fit into more than one category, but we only put each in one place on your list for your convenience. (Books that are part of a series are the one exception, as you may find an individual title in one spot and the whole series referenced elsewhere.) So if you're finding that you want to read more than one book from a particular challenge, the odds are good that skimming the list will give you another challenge to list it under. For instance, Where's the Big, Bad Wolf? from challenge 33 (a funny book) would also fit really well under challenge 34 (a mystery or detective story), challenge 15 (a book of fairy tales or folk tales), or challenge 62 (a book about animals). Shuffle things as you like!

A Variety of Reading Levels

Some of these books are clearly geared as a read-aloud at this age and would be challenging for most second-graders to read independently. However, most of the books do fall into the range of material typically suggested for a second grader. Our suggestion would be not to worry much about which books are read by your student vs. yourself. Grab the titles that interest you and him, and then flip through them. Which ones is he ready to enjoy reading? Set those aside for him. The rest you'll read to him. As your year progresses and his skills increase you'll likely find you are setting more and more books aside for him to read. Read-alouds meet your child's tremendous need for literacy, language, and stories though, so never shy away from simply reading to him!

A Note About Our Book Ideas

If you've been reading to your child long (or if you've simply perused your local public library) you've probably noticed that families have very different standards in their reading materials. The books you'll find listed here are ones that members of our team have read, added to their "I want to read this" list, or have had recommended to them.

Even among our team there is a wide range in what titles our families would find acceptable. Some of us find fantasy objectionable and would skip books that obscure a solid Christian worldview - but will gladly read a scarier adventure story than other families would be comfortable with. Others of us consider those fantasy titles to be an interesting addition and worthy of much discussion. We've opted to include titles with abandon, knowing that you will be able to flip through them at the library to determine if they are a good fit for your family.

So this is not a "Timberdoodle would sell these books if we could" list. We can't vouch for each of the titles, and we certainly can't know which ones are a good fit for your particular family. Mostly we're providing this list to give you some ideas, just in case you're drawing a blank in thinking of books for a particular topic. Use the ideas as a jumping-off point they are intended as, and, as always, we highly recommend previewing the books yourself.

Use Your Library
We can't overemphasize how useful your local library will be to you this year. We've listed multiple options under each challenge to try to ensure at least one title will be available. Now that most libraries allow you to place books on hold online, you'll find that you can use any spare hour in your day to request books for the next challenges and then whoever is in town next can swing by the library and pick them up. If you've not yet become a dedicated library user, this is the year!

Reading and Talking
If you're newer to reading together, our biggest tips for you are these. First, just read together. Whether you read a page or read a book you are making memories and building literacy. Don't overthink this - just squeeze it in as you can and watch reading time quickly become a highlight of your day.

Secondly, make sure you're discussing what you're reading. This doesn't need to be a formal book report on every book you encounter (please no!) or a tedious question and answer session every evening. Instead, talk as you go:

"Look at their faces! How do they feel? Why?"
"Do you like his choice? What would you do?"
"What do you think will happen next?"
"It looks like he thinks he is the most important. What's the truth?"
"What was your favorite part of this book?"

In these simple questions you are building emotional intelligence, worldview, logic, observational skills, and so much more.

Make This List Even Better
We love your book recommendations and feedback! Did you find a book you loved this year? We'd love to add your recommendations! Just shoot us a note at books@timberdoodle.com and let us know. Or perhaps you were disenchanted with one of our suggestions? Please let us know!

At the end of the year, fill out the Reader Awards on page 92 and submit that - we'll be thrilled to credit you 50 Doodle Dollar Reward points (worth $2.50 off your next order) as our thank you for taking the time to share.

512 READING CHALLENGE IDEAS, CONT.

1. A BOOK ABOUT BEING A CHRISTIAN OR ABOUT WHAT THE BIBLE TEACHES

The Ology: Ancient Truths Ever New by Marty Machowski
✓ *The Biggest Story* by Kevin DeYoung
The Gospel Story Bible by Marty Machowski
Wise Up by Marty Machowski
Big Beliefs by David R. Helm
Long Story Short by Marty Machowski
Old Story New by Marty Machowski
The Garden, the Curtain, and the Cross by Carl Laferton
The Tiny Truths Illustrated Bible by Joanna Rivard and Tim Penner

2. A BOOK ABOUT THE WORLD

A Ticket Around the World by Natalia Diaz
DK Children Just Like Me by Anabel Kindersley
This is the World by Miroslav Šašek
Little Kids First Big Book of the World by Elizabeth Carney
✓ *Usborne My Very First Our World Book*
Stories from Around the World by Heather Amery
This is How We Do It by Matt Lamothe
✓ *The Berenstain Bears Around the World* by Mike Berenstain

3. A BIOGRAPHY

Easy Reader Biographies from Scholastic
National Geographic Readers Bios
Christian Biographies for Young Readers series by Simonetta Carr
Childhood of Famous Americans series
✓ *The Story of Ruby Bridges* by Robert Coles
Abraham Lincoln by Ingri and Edgar Parin D'Aulaire

Leif the Lucky by Ingri and Edgar Parin D'Aulaire
Mary on Horseback by Rosemary Wells

✓ 4. A CLASSIC NOVEL/STORY

Little House series by Laura Ingalls Wilder
Betsy-Tacy series by Maud Hart Lovelace
The Swiss Family Robinson by Johann David Wyss
The Voyages of Doctor Doolittle by Hugh Lofting

✓ 5. A BOOK YOUR GRANDPARENT (OR OTHER RELATIVE) SAYS WAS HIS/HER FAVORITE AT YOUR AGE

Ask your grandparents or relatives. Or, if that's not possible, ask your Facebook friends for a recommendation for your child.

✓ 6. A BOOK FROM THE OLD TESTAMENT

This could be a literal book of the Old Testament, or it could be a book based on a section of the Old Testament.

7. A BOOK FROM THE NEW TESTAMENT

This could be a literal book of the New Testament, or it could be a book based on a section of the New Testament.

8. A BOOK BASED ON A TRUE STORY

Pocahontas: Princess of Faith and Courage by Maja Ledgerwood
✓ *Lucky Ducklings* by Eva Moore
The Big Balloon Race by Eleanor Coerr
Cora Frear by Susan E. Goodman
Riding the Pony Express by Clyde Robert Bulla
Keep the Lights Burning, Abbie by Connie Roop
The 18 Penny Goose by Sally M. Walker
Brave Girl by Michelle Markel
Warm as Wool by Scott Russell Sanders

9. A BOOK YOUR PASTOR OR SUNDAY SCHOOL TEACHER RECOMMENDS

Ask your pastor or Sunday School teacher - they will likely be thrilled to share a book they love.

10. A BOOK MORE THAN 100 YEARS OLD

Heidi by Johanna Spyri
The Wonderful Wizard of Oz by L. Frank Baum
The Wind in the Willows by Kenneth Grahame
✓ *Raggedy Ann Stories* by Johnny Gruelle

11. A BOOK ABOUT FAMILIES

✓ *The Little Brute Family* by Russell Hoban
Happy Little Family by Rebecca Caudill
The Vanderbeekeers of 141st Street by Karina Yan Glaser
The Littles series by John Peterson
Miracles on Maple Hill by Virginia Sorensen

12. A BOOK ABOUT RELATIONSHIPS OR FRIENDSHIP

Cul-de-Sac Kids series by Beverly Lewis
Sidney and Norman by Phil Vischer
✓ *One Cool Friend* by Toni Buzzeo
Betsy and Billy by Carolyn Haywood
Jake Drake series by Andrew Clements
Friendship According to Humphrey by Betty G. Birney
Chester's Way by Kevin Henkes

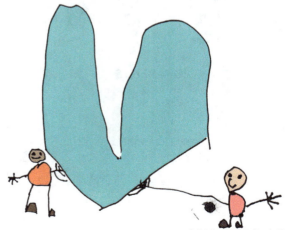

13. A BOOK FEATURING SOMEONE OF A DIFFERENT ETHNICITY THAN YOU

Anna Wang series by Andrea Cheng
Betsy and Tacy Go Over the Big Hill by Maud Hart Lovelace
Molly's Pilgrim by Barbara Cohen
Wagon Wheels by Barbara Brenner
✓ *Fly High!* by Louise Borden

14. A BOOK ABOUT SOMEONE WHO CAME FROM ANOTHER COUNTRY

✓ *All the Way to America* by Dan Yaccarino
The Long Way to a New Land by Joan Sandin
The Long Way Westward by Joan Sandin
A Different Pond by Bao Phi
My Name is Sangoel by Karen Williams
The Quiet Place by Sarah Stewart
Home at Last by Susan Middleton Elya
I'm New Here by Anne Sibley O'Brien

15. A BOOK OF FAIRY TALES OR FOLK TALES (OR AN EXTENDED RETELLING OF ONE)

Hans Christian Andersen's Fairy Tales
The Tall Book of Nursery Tales
A First Book of Fairy Tales
The King's Equal by Katherine Paterson
Fairy Tale Comics by Chris Duffy
The Talking Eggs by Robert D. San Souci
✓ *The Princess and the Pea* by Rachel Isadora

✓ 16. A BOOK RECOMMENDED BY A PARENT OR SIBLING

Encourage your child to ask his parents or siblings for a book recommendation. Or, if he prefers to choose his own titles, have him ask for a couple options from each and let him pick from that list.

✓
17. A BOOK BY OR ABOUT A MISSIONARY

Missionary Stories with the Millers by Mildred A. Martin
I Heard Good News Today by Cornelia Lehn
YWAM Heroes for Young Readers series
Granny Han's Breakfast by Sheila Groves
New Toes for Tia by Larry Dinkins
A Question of Yams by Gloria Repp

18. A CALDECOTT, NEWBERY, OR GEISEL AWARD WINNER

✓ *The Lion and the Mouse* by Jerry Pinkney
A Ball for Daisy by Chris Raschka
The One and Only Ivan by Katherine Applegate
So You Want to Be President? by Judith St. George
Zelda and Ivy: The Runaways by Laura McGee Kvasnosky

✓
19. A BOOK ABOUT A HOLIDAY

Christmas in the Big Woods by Laura Ingalls Wilder and Renee Graef
The Puppy Who Wanted a Boy by Jane Thayer
A Charlie Brown Christmas by Charles M. Schulz
Andi's Circle C Christmas by Susan K. Marlow
Cam Jansen: The Valentine Baby Mystery by David A. Adler
Sarah Gives Thanks by Mike Allegra
Cranberry series by Wende Devlin
The First Thanksgiving by Linda Hayward
The First Thanksgiving by Jean Craighead George
The Thanksgiving Story by Alice Dalgliesh
The Story of the Pilgrims by Katharine Ross
A Christmas Like Helen's by Natalie Kinsey-Warnock

20. A BOOK ABOUT GRANDPARENTS

✓ *No Kimchi for Me!* by Aram Kim
Nora's Ark by Natalie Kinsey-Warnock
Dear Juno by Soyung Pak
Henry and Mudge and the Great Grandpas by Cynthia Rylant
Gus and Grandpa by Claudia Mills

21. A BOOK WITH VISUAL PUZZLES

✓ *The Circus Ship* by Chris Van Dusen
Where's Waldo? books
I Spy books
Usborne 1001 Things to Spot books
Disney Look and Find books
Highlights Hidden Pictures books
Seek and Find Bible Stories by Carl Anker Mortensen

22. A BOOK THAT HAS A FRUIT OF THE SPIRIT IN ITS TITLE

✓ *Somebody Loves You, Mr. Hatch* by Eileen Spinelli
Princess Joy's Birthday Blessings by Jeanna Young and Jaqueline Johnson
The Berenstain Bears: Kindness Counts by Stan and Jan Berenstain
Little Critter: Just a Little Love by Mercer Mayer
The Berenstain Bears and the Joy of Giving by Stan and Jan Berenstain
Bob and Larry in the Case of the Missing Patience by Karen Poth

23. A BOOK ABOUT A FARM

✓ *Farmer Duck* by Martin Waddell
Duck to the Rescue by John Himmelman
Old MacDonald Had a Truck by Steve Goetz
My Big Wimmelbook: On the Farm by Max Walther
The Berenstain Bears Down on the Farm by Stan and Jan Berenstain

24. A BOOK ABOUT ILLNESS OR MEDICINE

Calling Doctor Amelia Bedelia by Herman Parish
A Sick Day for Amos McGee by Philip C. Stead
Mr. Putter and Tabby Catch the Cold by Cynthia Rylant
Brave Clara Barton by Frank Murphy
✓ *Florence Nightingale* by Demi

25. A BOOK ABOUT SCHOOL OR LEARNING

Teach Us, Amelia Bedelia by Peggy Parish
Andi's Scary School Days by Susan K. Marlow
Mr. Putter and Tabby Ring the Bell by Cynthia Rylant
✓ *This Is My Home, This Is My School* by Jonathan Bean
"B" Is for Betsy by Carolyn Haywood
Skippack School by Marguerite De Angeli
The Littles Go to School by John Peterson
School Days According to Humphrey by Betty G. Birney

✓ 26. A GRAPHIC NOVEL

Toon Into Reading series
First Graphics: My Community series by Lori Mortensen and others
Pet Shop Private Eye series by Colleen Venable
Mr. Badger and Mrs. Fox series by Brigitte Luciani
Owly series by Andy Runton
Or check our website for other series we love!

27. A BOOK OF POETRY

Where the Sidewalk Ends by Shel Silverstein
Something Big Has Been Here by Jack Prelutsky
Surprises by Lee Bennett Hopkins
✓ *The Llama Who Had No Pajama* by Mary Ann Hoberman
Favorite Poems of Childhood by Philip Smith
The Oxford Illustrated Book of American Children's Poems
Julie Andrews' Collection of Poems, Songs, and Lullabies
The 20th Century Children's Poetry Treasury selected by Jack Prelutsky

✓ 28. A BOOK WITH A GREAT COVER

Let your child choose–it will be interesting to see what he considers to be a great cover!

29. A BOOK ABOUT FOOD

Seven Loaves of Bread by Ferida Wolff
Fox and Crow Are Not Friends by Melissa Wiley
D.W. the Picky Eater by Marc Brown
Stick Dog by Tom Watson
✓*Tales for Very Picky Eaters* by Josh Schneider
✓*The Best Chef in Second Grade* by Katharine Kenah

30. A BOOK ABOUT WEATHER

Henry and Mudge and the Wild Wind by Cynthia Rylant
✓*Thunder Cake* by Patricia Polacco
Mr. Putter and Tabby Hit the Slope by Cynthia Rylant
Ling and Ting: Together in All Weather by Grace Lin
The Littles and the Big Storm by John Peterson
Weather by Lee Bennett Hopkins
I Spy Up in the Sky The Clouds by Tamra Orr
Come On, Rain! by Karen Hesse
Storm in the Night by Mary Stolz
Oh Say Can You Say What's the Weather Today? by Tish Rabe

✓31. A BOOK ABOUT AN ADVENTURE

The Bears on Hemlock Mountain by Alice Dalgliesh
Mice of the Westing Wind series by Tim Davis
The Adventures of Benny and Watch series by Gertrude Chandler Warner and Daniel Mark Duffy
Otis and Will Discover the Deep by Barb Rosenstock
Mac B., Kid Spy series by Mac Barnett

32. A BOOK BY OR ABOUT WILLIAM SHAKESPEARE

A Stage Full of Shakespeare Stories by Angela McAllister
Graphic Shakespeare
✓*Bard of Avon* by Diane Stanley
William Shakespeare and the Globe by Aliki
Will's Words by Jane Sutcliffe
Mr. Shakepeare's Plays by Marcia Williams
Usborne Illustrated Stories from Shakespeare

✓33. A FUNNY BOOK

Parents in the Pigpen, Pigs in the Tub by Amy Ehrlich
Where's the Big Bad Wolf? by Eileen Christelow
Tales from Deckawoo Drive series by Kate DiCamillo
Pippi Longstocking by Astrid Lingren
Mercy Watson series by Kate DiCamillo

34. A MYSTERY OR DETECTIVE STORY

Scripture Sleuth series by Mat Halverson
The Berenstain Bears and the Missing Honey by Stan and Jan Berenstain
The Happy Hollisters series by Jerry West
The Bobbsey Twins series by Laura Lee Hope
✓*A to Z Mysteries* series by Ron Roy
✓*The Zach and Zoe Mysteries* series by Mike Lupica

✓35. AN EASY READER CLASSIC

The Cat in the Hat by Dr Seuss
Little Bear series by Else Holmelund Minarik
Frog and Toad series and others by Arnold Lobel

Frances series by Russell Hoban
Berenstain Bears Inside Outside Upside Down by Stan and
  Jan Berenstain

✓ ## 36. A BOOK BY OR ABOUT A FAMOUS AMERICAN
Harriet Tubman: Freedom Fighter by Nadia L. Hohn
Alexander Hamilton: A Plan for America by Sarah Albee
Martin Luther King Jr.: A Peaceful Leader by Sarah Albee
George Washington: The First President by Sarah Albee
Long, Tall Lincoln by Jennifer Dussling
John F. Kennedy the Brave by Sheila Keenan
Childhood of Famous Americans Ready-to-Read series
Abe Lincoln's Hat by Martha Brenner

37. A BOOK ABOUT ANCIENT HISTORY
Pompeii: Buried Alive! by Edith Kunhardt
Viking Adventure by Clyde Robert Bulla
Tut's Mummy Lost and Found by Judy Donnelly
Archaeologists Dig for Clues by Kate Duke
The Usborne Time Traveler
Cleopatra by Diane Stanley
✓ *Usborne Book of World History*

✓ ## 38. A BOOK ABOUT MEDIEVAL HISTORY
Castle Diary by Richard Platt
The Sword in the Tree by Robert Clyde Bulla
Tales of Robin Hood by Tony Allan
Joan of Arc by Diane Stanley
Good Queen Bess by Diane Stanley
Marguerite Makes a Book by Bruce Robertson
The Knight and the Dragon by Tomie dePaola
The Hawk of the Castle by Danna Smith
The Knight at Dawn by Mary Pope Osborne
Knights by Philip Steele
Princess of the Reformation: Jeanne D'Albret by Rebekah Dan

39. A BOOK ABOUT MONEY
Arthur's Funny Money by Lillian Hoban
A Bargain for Frances by Russell Hoban
Little Critter: Just Saving My Money by Mercer Mayer
The Berenstain Bears Piggy Bank Blessings by Stan and Jan
  Berenstain with Mike Berenstain
The Tuttle Twins and the Food Truck Fiasco by Connor Boyack
Fox on the Job by James Marshall
Follow the Money by Loreen Leedy
✓ *Alexander, Who Used to Be Rich Last Sunday* by Judith Viorst
One Cent, Two Cents, Old Cent, New Cent by Bonnie Worth

40. A BOOK ABOUT ART OR ARTISTS
Katie series by James Mayhew
Famous Children series by Tony Hart
Getting to Know the World's Greatest Artists series by
  Mike Venezia
Come Look with Me series
Artists Books for Children series by Laurence Anholt
How Artists See series by Colleen Carroll
My Little Artist by Donna Green
✓ *The Chalk Box Kid* by Clyde Robert Bulla
The Paint Brush Kid by Clyde Robert Bulla

41. A BOOK ABOUT MUSIC OR A MUSICIAN

Composer series by Anna Harwell Celenza
Sing to the Stars by Mary Brigid Barrett
A Band of Angels by Deborah Hopkinson
✓ *Mr. Putter and Tabby Toot the Horn* by Cynthia Rylant
Mole Music by David McPhail
Max Found Two Sticks by Brian Pinkney
Francis Scott Key's Star-Spangled Banner by Monica Kulling

42. A BOOK ABOUT AN INVENTION OR INVENTOR

How Things Are Made by Oldrich Ruzicka
The Boo-Boos That Changed the World: A True Story About an Accidental Invention (Really!) by Barry Wittenstein
Ben Franklin Thinks Big by Sheila Keenan
First Flight by George Shea
The Story of Paper by Ying Chang Compestine
✓ *Balloons Over Broadway* by Melissa Sweet
Oh, the Things They Invented! by Bonnie Worth

43. A BOOK ABOUT FEELINGS OR EMOTIONS

Listening to My Body by Gabi Garcia
Alexander and the Terrible, Horrible, No Good, Very Bad Day by Judith Viorst
✓ *Jabari Jumps* by Gaia Cornwall
A Whole Bunch of Feelings by Jennifer Moore-Mallinos

44. A BOOK ABOUT A BOY

Henry and Mudge series by Cynthia Rylant
Arthur series by Marc Brown
Nate the Great series by Marjorie Wieman Sharmat
✓ *My Father's Dragon* by Ruth Stiles Gannett
Flat Stanley by Jeff Brown
Here's Hank by Henry Winkler
Billy and Blaze series by C.W. Anderson
Harry Miller's Run by David Almond

✓ 45. A BOOK ABOUT A GIRL

Gooney Bird Greene series by Lois Lowry
Little House in the Big Woods by Laura Ingalls Wilder
Ramona books by Beverly Cleary
Nancy Clancy series by Jane O'Connor
Ruthie's Gift by Kimberly Brubaker Bradley
Amazing Grace by Mary Hoffman
Kenna Ford and the Second Grade Mix-up by Melissa Thomson
Cowgirl Kate and Cocoa series by Erica Silverman

46. A BOOK ABOUT BOOKS OR A LIBRARY
Lumber Camp Library by Natalie Kinsey-Warnock
Amelia Bedelia, Bookworm by Herman Parish
Least of All by Carol Purdy
Clara and the Bookwagon by Nancy Smiler Levinson
Mr. George Baker by Amy Hest
Mr. Putter and Tabby Turn the Page by Cynthia Rylant
✓*That Book Woman* by Heather Henson

✓ 47. A BOOK ABOUT ADOPTION
Through Moon and Stars and Night Skies by Ann Turner
I Don't Have Your Eyes by Carrie A. Kitze
Penny and Peter by Carolyn Haywood
Here's a Penny by Carolyn Haywood
The Mulberry Bird by Anne Braff Brodzinsky

48. A BOOK ABOUT SOMEONE WHO IS DIFFERENTLY ABLED
✓*Just Because* by Rebecca Elliott
A Splash of Red by Jen Bryant
A Boy and a Jaguar by Alan Rabinowitz
My Brother Charlie by Holly Robinson Peete and Ryan Elizabeth Peete
Helen's Big World by Doreen Rappaport
Six Dots by Jen Bryant

49. A BOOK YOU OR YOUR FAMILY OWNS BUT YOU'VE NEVER READ
If you're a responsible person who has read every book in the house, feel free to use a book you've walked past at the library or a book your child has heard people talking about but never read.

✓ 50. A BOOK ABOUT BABIES
The Year of the Baby by Andrea Cheng
Betsy's Little Star by Carolyn Haywood
Amelia Bedelia and the Baby by Peggy Parish
The New Small Person by Lauren Child
Once Upon a Baby Brother by Sarah Sullivan

51. A BOOK ABOUT WRITING
Mr. Putter and Tabby Write the Book by Cynthia Rylant
The Right Word: Roget and His Thesaurus by Jen Bryant
Nancy Clancy: Late-Breaking News by Jane O'Connor
✓*Home Work* by Arthur Yoinks
Ralph Tells a Story by Abby Hanlon
The Best Story by Eileen Spinelli
Little Red Writing by Joan Holub
What Do Authors Do? by Eileen Christelow

52. A BOOK MADE INTO A MOVIE
✓*Charlotte's Web* by E.B. White
Cloudy with a Chance of Meatballs by Judi Barrett
A Bear Called Paddington by Michael Bond
Meet Felicity: An American Girl by Valerie Tripp
The Rescuers by Margery Sharp

✓ 53. A BOOK ABOUT PRAYER
What Every Child Should Know About Prayer by Nancy Guthrie
The Berenstain Bears Say Their Prayers by Stan and Jan Berenstain with Mike Berenstain

From Akebu to Zapotec by June Hathersmith
What Happens When I Talk to God? by Stormie Omartian
Asking Father by E. & L. Harvey and Trudy Tait
There's No Wrong Way to Pray by Rebecca Ninke and Kate E.H. Watson

54. A BOOK RECOMMENDED BY A LIBRARIAN OR TEACHER

Ask your librarian, ballet teacher, karate instructor, Sunday School teacher...

✓ 55. AN ENCYCLOPEDIA, DICTIONARY OR ALMANAC

This is unlikely to be a book you'll read cover-to-cover, yet it's definitely a resource you want your child to be familiar with. Consider reading a set number of pages or spending a specified amount of time and then checking it off the list.

✓ *Usborne Children's Encyclopedia*
Scholastic Children's Encyclopedia
DK Smithsonian Picturepedia
DK Merriam-Webster's Children's Dictionary

56. A BOOK ABOUT BUILDING OR ARCHITECTURE

Amelia Bedelia Under Construction by Herman Parish
The Ultimate Construction Site Book by Anne-Sophie Baumann
My Big Wimmelbook: At the Construction Site by Max Walther
Look at That Building! by Scot Ritchie
Roberto: The Insect Architect by Nina Laden
Angelo by David Macaulay

57. A BIOGRAPHY OF A WORLD LEADER

Nelson Mandela: From Prisoner to President by Suzy Capozzi
Martin's Big Words: The Life of Dr. Martin Luther King, Jr. by Doreen Rappaport
Malala's Magic Pencil by Malala Yousafzai
Peter the Great by Diane Stanley
✓ *To Dare Mighty Things: The Life of Theodore Roosevelt* by Doreen Rappaport

✓ 58. A BOOK PUBLISHED THE SAME YEAR YOUR FIRST GRADER WAS BORN

You choose. Stumped? We found that searching for "best childrens' books of 20__" provided several lists to browse.

EXTRA YARN

59. A BOOK WITH A ONE-WORD TITLE

Madeline by Ludwig Bemelmans
Tornado by Betsy Byars
Bandit by Karen Rostoker-Gruber
✓ *Pond* by Jim LaMarche
Begin by Philip Ulrich

60. A BOOK ABOUT SERVICE

✓ *The Giving Tree* by Shel Silverstein
Tea Cakes for Tosh by Kelly Starling Lyons
A Castle on Viola Street by DyAnne DiSalvo
The Lady in the Box by Ann McGovern

61. A BOOK ABOUT SIBLINGS

Dick and Jane books
Ling and Ting series by Grace Lin
Do Like Kyla by Angela Johnson
Tales of Amanda Pig by Jean Van Leeuwen
✓ *Louise Loves Art* by Kelly Light
Best Friends for Frances by Russell Hoban

✓ 62. A BOOK ABOUT ANIMALS

The Ant and the Elephant by Bill Peet
Andi's Fair Surprise by Susan K. Marlow
Mountain Born by Elizabeth Yates
Lulu series by Hilary McKay

Step Right Up by Donna Janell Bowman
James Herriot's Treasury for Children

✓ 63. A BOOK FEATURING A DOG

Absolutely Lucy by Ilene Cooper
Tippy Lemmey by Patricia C. McKissack
The Bravest Dog Ever: The True Story of Balto by Natalie Standiford
Five True Dog Stories by Margaret Davidson
Dogku by Andrew Clements
If I Ran the Dog Show by Tish Rabe
Ribsy by Beverly Cleary

✓ 64. A BOOK FEATURING A CAT

The Fire Cat by Esther Averill
The Last Little Cat by Meindert DeJong
Cam Jansen: The Catnapping Mystery by David A. Adler
The Case of the Cat's Meow by Crosby Bonsall
Otis and the Kittens by Loren Long
What Cat is That? by Tish Rabe
My Pet Human by Yasmine Surovec

✓ 65. A WORDLESS BOOK

Harold and the Purple Crayon by Crockett Johnson
Little Fox in the Forest by Stephanie Graegin
Wolf in the Snow by Matthew Cordell
Noah's Ark by Peter Spier
Ah-Choo by Mercer Mayer

✓ 66. A BOOK ABOUT PLANTS OR GARDENING

Mercy Watson Thinks Like a Pig by Kate DiCamillo
The Gardener by Sarah Stewart
Oswald's Garden by Heather Feldman
The Friendship Garden series by Jenny Meyerhoff
The Vanderbeekers and the Hidden Garden by Karina Yan Glaser
Up in the Garden and Down in the Dirt by Kate Messner

67. A BOOK ABOUT A HOBBY OR A SKILL YOU WANT TO LEARN

You choose - is there something that your child would enjoy learning? From science experiments to building a fort, there's a book for everything. Keep in mind that the skill doesn't have to be feasible to use right away. Choosing a horse or flying a space ship are fair game!

68. A BOOK OF COMICS

Peanuts by Charles Schulz
✓ *Family Circus* by Bil Keane
✓ *Calvin and Hobbes* by Bill Watterson
The Adventures of Tintin by Herge
Red and Rover by Brian Basset

69. A BOOK ABOUT A FAMOUS WAR

Twenty and Ten by Claire Hutchet Bishop
Pink and Say by Patricia Polacco
Primrose Day by Carolyn Haywood
Welcome to Molly's World by Catherine Gourley
Revolutionary War on Wednesday by Mary Pope Osborne
✓ *Civil War on Sunday* by Mary Pope Osborne

70. A BOOK ABOUT SPORTS

Mr. Putter and Tabby Drop the Ball by Cynthia Rylant
Pass the Ball, Mo! by David A. Adler
The Berenstain Bears Play Ball by Stan and Jan Berenstain
Betsy and the Boys by Carolyn Haywood
Brothers at Bat by Audrey Vernick
Cam Jansen: The Sport Day Mysteries by David A. Adler
The Streak by Barb Rosenstock

71. A BOOK ABOUT MATH

Ben Franklin and the Magic Squares by Frank Murphy
Life of Fred series
A Hundred Billion Trillion Stars by Seth Fishman
Mystery Math by David A. Adler
Sir Cumference series by Cindy Neuschwander
The Lion's Share by Matthew McElligott
One Grain of Rice by Demi
The Girl With a Mind for Math by Julia Finley Mosca

72. A BOOK ABOUT SUFFERING OR POVERTY

✓ *The Hundred Dresses* by Eleanor Estes
Henry's Freedom Box by Ellen Levine
Dust for Dinner by Ann Turner
The Patchwork Bike by Maxine Beneba Clarke
I Am a Bear by Jean-Francois Dumont

✓ 73. A BOOK BY YOUR FAVORITE AUTHOR

Your child will choose this one, though you may have to help him think through his favorite books to narrow down the author he's enjoying most right now.

74. A BOOK YOU'VE READ BEFORE

Your child should choose, and make sure you mark it down since it's obviously one he finds interesting!

75. A BOOK WITH AN UGLY COVER

Let your child choose, of course, and make sure to document what he thinks is ugly about it!

76. A CHRISTIAN NOVEL

Circle C Beginnings novels by Susan K. Marlow
The Adventures of Adam Raccoon by Glen Keane
Sugar Creek Gang series by Paul Hutchens
Imagination Station series by Adventures in Odyssey

77. A BOOK ABOUT TRAVEL OR TRANSPORTATION

Mercy Watson Goes for a Ride by Kate DiCamillo
✓ *Let's Go for a Drive* by Mo Willems
LaRue Across America by Mark Teague
The Relatives Came by Cynthia Rylant
Arthur's Family Vacation by Marc Brown
On the Road by Lucy Nolan
Road Trip by Roger Eschbacher

78. A BOOK ABOUT THE NATURAL WORLD

✓ *The Boy Who Drew Birds* by Jacqueline Davies
Sky Tree by Thomas Locker
Pony Scouts: The Camping Trip by Catherine Hapka

Old Mother West Wind by Thorton W. Burgess
The Camping Trip that Changed America by Barb Rosenstock
Over and Under the Pond by Kate Messner
A Camping Spree with Mr. Magee by Chris Van Dusen

79. A BIOGRAPHY OF AN AUTHOR

Big Machines: The Story of Virginia Lee Burton by Sherri Duskey Rinker
⊘ *A Boy, a Mouse, and a Spider--The Story of E. B. White* by Barbara Herkert
John Ronald's Dragons: The Story of J. R. R. Tolkien by Caroline McAlister
Noah Webster's Fighting Words by Tracy Nelson Maurer
Ordinary, Extraordinary Jane Austen by Deborah Hopkinson
A Boy Called Dickens by Deborah Hopkinson

80. A BOOK PUBLISHED IN 2019-2020   JUST ASK

Your librarian should be able to point you towards the new releases that are age-appropriate (you may want to preview them, though!) or you can watch to see what's being featured in your favorite book-seller's email or storefront. Of course, you could also expand this category to be any brand-new book or new-to-your-library title.

81. A HISTORICAL FICTION BOOK

✓ *The Whipping Boy* by Sid Fleischman
The Courage of Sarah Noble by Alice Dalgleish
Thee Hannah! by Marguerite de Angeli
Clipper Ship by Thomas P. Lewis
Sam the Minuteman by Nathaniel Benchley
Prairie Friends by Nancy Smiler Levinson
Daniel's Duck by Clyde Robert Bulla
Magic Treehouse series by Mary Pope Osborne

82. A BOOK ABOUT SCIENCE OR A SCIENTIST

✓ *Indescribable* by Louie Giglio
Greg's Microscope by Millicent E. Selsam
Magic School Bus books by Joanna Cole
Wells of Knowledge Science Series
Mesmerized by Mara Rockliff
Wile E. Coyote Physical Science series
Solving the Puzzle Under the Sea by Robert Burleigh
Ada Twist, Scientist by Andrea Beaty

83. A BOOK ABOUT SAFETY OR SURVIVAL

Do your kids know both when and how to call 911? As landlines become less common, you will want to make sure that your child knows how to access 911 on the actual devices he has access to everyday. You won't see that specifically addressed in these books but it is worth setting some time aside to discuss this with your child. (BTW, if you accidentally actually dial 911 stay on the line. Every department is different, but here our police department is obligated to investigate every 911 hang-up for obvious reasons but if you stay on the line and explain that will save everyone some time.)

This is also a great opportunity to visit your local fire and police departments for a tour. Your child will learn a ton about his community, and they often have helpful handouts for instance, fire escape planning info, etc.

Kids to the Rescue! by Maribeth Boelts
I Can Be Safe by Pat Thomas
Officer Buckle and Gloria by Peggy Rathmann
Arthur's Fire Drill by Marc Brown
I Survived series by Lauren Tarshis
First Aid Basics by Elizabeth Lang

84. A BOOK ABOUT SPACE OR AN ASTRONAUT

Mr. Putter and Tabby See the Stars by Cynthia Rylant
Moonwalk: The First Trip to the Moon by Judy Donnelly
Mae Among the Stars by Roda Ahmed
Caroline's Comets by Emily Arnold McCully
The Magic School Bus Lost in the Solar System by Joanna Cole

85. A BOOK SET IN CENTRAL OR SOUTH AMERICA
Hill of Fire by Thomas P. Lewis
A Bear for Miguel by Elaine Marie Alphin
Ada's Violin by Susan Hood
Love and Roast Chicken by Barbara Knutson
✓ *Waiting for the Biblioburro* by Monica Brown
Ready to Read: Living in Brazil by Chloe Perkins
Ready to Read: Living in Mexico by Chloe Perkins
The Amazing Mexico Secret by Jeff Brown and Macky Pamintuan

86. A BOOK SET IN AFRICA
Anna Hibiscus series by Atinuke
✓ *Uncommon Traveler* by Don Brown
Mama Miti by Donna Jo Napoli
Mufaro's Beautiful Daughters by John Steptoe

Safari, So Good! by Bonnie Worth
Ready to Read: Living in South Africa by Chloe Perkins
The African Safari Discovery by Jeff Brown and Macky Pamintuan

✓ 87. A BOOK SET IN ASIA
The Whispering Cloth by Pegi Deitz Shea
The Story About Ping by Marjorie Flack
✓ *Tikki Tikki Tembo* by Arlene Mosel
A Grain of Rice by Helena Clare Pittman
Ready to Read: Living in China by Chloe Perkins
Ready to Read: Living in India by Chloe Perkins
Ready to Read: Living in South Korea by Chloe Perkins
The Chinese Flying Wonders by Jeff Brown and Macky Pamintuan

88. A BOOK SET IN EUROPE
Madeline series by Ludwig Bemelmans
The Martha Years series by Melissa Wiley
The House on Walenska Street by Charlotte Herman
Ready to Read: Living in Italy by Chloe Perkins
A Walk in London by Salvatore Rubbino
Framed in France by Jeff Brown and Macky Pamintuan

✓ 89. A BOOK WITH A COLOR IN ITS TITLE
The Yellow House Mystery by Gertrude Chandler Warner
Blue Bay Mystery by Gertrude Chandler Warner
Encyclopedia Brown series by Donald J. Sobol
The Green Ember series by S.D. Smith

90. A BOOK ABOUT MANNERS
Dear Mr. Washington by Lynn Cullen
Do Unto Otters by Laurie Keller
How Do Dinosaurs Eat Their Food? by Jane Yolen
✓ *Mind Your Manners, B.B. Wolf* by Judy Sierra

91. A BOOK ABOUT SPRING

Spring According to Humphrey by Betty G. Birney
The Adventures of Peter Cottontail and His Green Forest Friends by Thornton Burgess
The Seasons Sewn: A Year in Patchwork by Ann Whitford Paul
Hickory by Palmer Brown
When Spring Comes by Keving Henkes
Mud Flat April Fool by James Stevenson
Robins! How They Grow Up by Eileen Christelow

√ 92. A BOOK ABOUT SUMMER

Andi's Indian Summer by Susan K. Marlow
The Summer Camp Mysteries by David A. Adler
Summer According to Humphrey by Betty G. Birney
Fireflies by Julie Brinckloe
Amanda Pig and the Really Hot Day by Jean Van Leeuwen

√ 93. A BOOK ABOUT AUTUMN

The Friendship Garden: Pumpkin Spice by Jenny Meyerhoff
Apple Cider-Making Days by Ann Purmell
Flora's Very Windy Day by Jeanne Birdsall

√ 94. A BOOK ABOUT WINTER

Snowshoe Thompson by Nancy Smiler Levinson
The Happy Hollisters at Snowflake Camp by Jerry West
Cam Jansen: The Snowy Day Mystery by David A. Adler
Winter According to Humphrey by Betty G. Birney
It's Snowing! It's Snowing! by Jack Prelutsky
Over and Under the Snow by Kate Messner

95. A BOOK FROM THE 000 DEWEY DECIMAL SECTION YOUR LIBRARY

Books about computer science, information and general works

√ 96. A BOOK FROM THE 100 DEWEY DECIMAL SECTION YOUR LIBRARY

Books about philosophy and psychology

√ 97. A BOOK FROM THE 200 DEWEY DECIMAL SECTION YOUR LIBRARY

Books about religion

✓ **98. A BOOK FROM THE 300 DEWEY DECIMAL SECTION YOUR LIBRARY**

Books about social sciences

99. A BOOK FROM THE 400 DEWEY DECIMAL SECTION YOUR LIBRARY

Books about language

100. A BOOK FROM THE 500 DEWEY DECIMAL SECTION YOUR LIBRARY

Books about science

101. A BOOK FROM THE 600 DEWEY DECIMAL SECTION YOUR LIBRARY

Books about technology

102. A BOOK FROM THE 700 DEWEY DECIMAL SECTION YOUR LIBRARY

Books about arts and recreation

103. A BOOK FROM THE 800 DEWEY DECIMAL SECTION YOUR LIBRARY

Books about literature

104. A BOOK FROM THE 900 DEWEY DECIMAL SECTION YOUR LIBRARY

Books about history and geography

BOOK AWARDS & PARTY!

DO THIS AS SOON AS YOU FINISH YOUR READING CHALLENGE!

Grab your child's reading list from pages 24-29 and help him fill out the awards page (opposite page) to give his best and worst books an official award and mark them as most memorable this year.

Encourage him not to agonize over "was this one really the best..." but to go with his general impressions or write down all the contenders.

Send us a copy of this at books@timberdoodle.com and we'll be thrilled to credit you 50 Doodle Dollar Reward points (worth $2.50 off your next order) as our thank you for taking the time to share. We'll also congratulate your child on a job so well done!

Bonus Idea
Have an "awards ceremony" night all about one of the books on your list! You'll get the most specific ideas by searching online for "*book I picked* theme party," but here's some things to think through as you get started.

Food: How can you tie the menu to the theme? A book like Green Eggs and Ham, Pancakes for Breakfast, or is easy - just replicate the food in the book! If you're working with a book that doesn't feature food directly there are a few options. Perhaps the book featured a construction crew - you could all eat from "lunchboxes" tonight, or set up your kitchen to masquerade as a food truck. Or if you're reading a book about the pioneers - do a little research and eat frying pan bread, beans, venison, and cornmeal mush.

You could also take the food you would normally eat and reshape it to match your story. For instance, sandwiches can be cut into ships, round apple slices can be life preservers, crackers labeled "hard tack," and you're well on your way to a party featuring your favorite nautical tale.

Don't forget the setting, too. As ridiculous as it sounds, eating dinner by (battery-operated!) lantern light under your table draped with blankets will make that simple camping tale an experience your family will be recalling for years to come.

Or perhaps some handmade red table fans, softly playing traditional Chinese music, and a red tablecloth would provide the perfect backdrop for the story about life in China.

The more senses you use, the more memorable you make this experience. Use appropriate background music, diffuse peppermint oil to make it smell like Christmas, dim the lights, eat at the top of the playground, or whatever would set this apart from a regular night and make it just a bit crazy and fun.

Don't get trapped in either the "we must do this tonight" mode or in the "we can't do this because it won't be perfect" mode. Allowing your child to spend a few days creating decorations and menus is wonderful! Doing it today because it's the only free night on the horizon even though you can only integrate a few ideas into the preset menu? Also amazing. Your goal is to value the book and make some fun memories.

BOOK AWARDS OF

I READ ___ BOOKS FROM THE READING CHALLENGE THIS YEAR!

FUNNIEST BOOK:

MOST MEMORABLE BOOK:

BOOK I READ THE MOST TIMES:

BOOK I LEAST ENJOYED:

TEACHER'S FAVORITE BOOK:

BOOK I MOST WISH WAS A SERIES:

CHOOSE YOUR OWN AWARD:

36 WAYS TO PLAY WITH MAD MATTR!

#1. Spoons & Forks
Use an assortment of silverware when playing with Mad Mattr this week. Can you make smooth paths with a spoon and curious holes with the forks? Which would you use to draw grass next to your road?

#2. Cookie Cutters
Roll your "cookie dough" out and use cookie cutters to make all sorts of "yummy cookies." Don't forget to sprinkle a little loose Mad Mattr on top of the finished product!

#3. Construction
Grab your smallest construction toys and use your bulldozers to push the "dirt" into piles or the backhoe to scoop it into dump trucks. Don't have any toys the right size? Spend your time making stacks of logs, piles of rocks, and other construction-themed resources.

#4. Cubes & Bricks
Using the table, can you make cubes with Mad Mattr? This takes a little practice, but it is very rewarding once mastered! Using your new cube skills, make bricks and build them into a wall. Too hard? Make a long "brick" and let your child use a knife to chop it into reasonable proportions.

#5. Pizza!
Squish about half of your Mad Mattr into a circle on the table. Roll much of what's left into a tube and slice it into "pepperoni" slices. Place them on the pizza, then sprinkle the rest of the Mad Mattr on top as cheese. Slice and serve!

#6. Archaeologist
Bury a toy animal or vehicle in Mad Mattr, then have your child use a spoon to "excavate" the archaeological find and reveal his treasure.

#7. Let It Snow!
This is a snow week. Can you make a snowman? Reserve a little Mad Mattr to sprinkle over the finished scene–it's still snowing!

#8. Eggs
With Mad Mattr's unique texture, this is one activity that really works well only for it. Squish all of your Mad Mattr into egg shapes, making sure to press them firmly together. You want them to be very hard and compacted. Grab a sturdy bowl and "crack" the eggs on the side of it. Then gently separate the two halves. (You can also break them apart by holding a half in each hand and separating.) Depending on your technique, you could get a clean break or, better yet, two halves with "liquid" Mad Mattr streaming down.

#9. Footprints
Go through your toy box and pull out any animals or dolls with interesting feet. Help them "walk" through Mad Mattr, using firm pressure to get good impressions. What do you notice? Can you tell which animal left which tracks?

#10. Hamburgers & Sandwich Cookies
Use your favorite cookie cutter and slice three identical cookies. Stack them up to make sandwich cookies. Next, grab a circle-shaped cutter (or biscuit cutter or drinking glass) and cut at least three of those. They will become your hamburger and bun. Can you add a slice of cheese, tomato, lettuce, etc?

#11. Bag It
Use a clean paper bag or box for today's Mad Mattr. Make holes for your child to put his hands through, and tape the top closed so he can't see inside. What can he make using only his hands and not his eyes? Make a few balls or cubes and put them in his bag. Can he tell which shape they are? How many does he have?

#12. Dinner Is Served
Shape Mad Mattr into a complete meal, and "serve" it on your child's regular dinner plate. Chicken and mashed potatoes will be easier to make than spaghetti and corn!

#13. Treasure Chests
Have your child find tiny toys and trinkets around the house, then encase them in Mad Mattr. Can he remember which item is where? (Mad Mattr is silicone-based, so stay away from other silicone items to avoid excessive sticking.)

#14. Money
If your child is past the choking hazard stage, raid your change bucket for coins. Use them to make imprints in Mad Mattr. Use the sides of the coins to make tracks, too!

#15. Snake Fossils
Find long objects around the house to use as your snakes. These could be dead headphone cables, charger cords for devices you no longer own, or even clean branches or vines. Create a stone slab with your Mad Mattr and arrange the "snake" of choice on the table. Then, press your stone over the snake firmly, creating a complete impression. Flip it over, remove the cord, and admire the imprint!

#16. Writing
Form your Mad Mattr into tablets, then use a pencil or stylus to inscribe letters or draw pictures.

#17. Beehive
You'll need a pencil and a couple of toothpicks or spaghetti noodles for this activity. Break the toothpicks/noodles in half for "bees"–you could even color them if you like. Now shape your Mad Mattr into tall beehives. Use your pencil to poke holes all the way through the Mad Mattr. Now your bees can go in and out of their hive!

#18. Make Bread
Knead the Mad Mattr and fold it into a loaf. While it "cooks" make a stick of pretend butter. Then slice the bread and top it with a slice of butter. Yum!

#19. Baked Potatoes
First, form potatoes out of Mad Mattr. Then, use a fork to poke them all over. While they are "baking," make a stick of butter and slice it. When the potatoes are done, slice them,

top them with butter, and serve!

#20. Hammer & Nails
Help your child draw windows, doors, walls, roofs, etc. on scraps of paper. Then, using a toy hammer and toothpicks, hammer the toothpicks through the paper and into a blob of Mad Mattr to make a house. Variations: Use a can or rock instead of a hammer. Draw parts of a backhoe, ambulance, or garden instead of parts of a house.

#21. Scissors
Spread your Mad Mattr as thin as possible while still keeping it thick enough to pick up. Have your child use his scissors to chop it up. You could even use a pencil to draw coupons into the Mad Mattr, then have him cut them out for you. (Or you could draw animals to cut out– the sky is the limit!)

#22. Apple Pie, Anyone?
Using a small bowl as a pie dish, press about a third of your Mad Mattr into it as a pie crust. Take about two-thirds of what is left and shape it into an apple or two, then let your child chop it up with a butter knife and fill the pie. Finally, form the remaining Mad Mattr into strips and lay them across your pie. Enjoy!

#23. Cookie Cutter Picture
Roll out your Mad Mattr, but instead of cutting it with a cookie cutter, just press it part way down, leaving an impression. What kind of scene can you make?

#24. Math
This week use Mad Mattr to answer as many questions as possible in your math book. Don't just talk about having five apples, then adding two more, but take the time to

actually make them. This can breathe new life into math, if the subject has become dull. It can also help clarify a new concept.

#25. Textures
Today is all about textures. Split your Mad Mattr into small sample swatches and smooth them each out. Then try pressing different items into your Mad Mattr, from thumbprints to clean leaves or colanders. What's the most interesting imprint?

#26. Dessert Extravaganza
This week make every kind of dessert you can think of, from chocolate truffles to cupcakes to shortbread cookies.

#27. Gardener's Delight
Take about half of your Mad Mattr and create a garden plot. This could be as simple as an uneven patch of ground or as elaborate as a "raised bed" rectangle. Now use the rest of your Mad Mattr to make flowers or vegetable plants for your garden.

#28. Finish the Picture
Using an interesting page from any book you have on hand, (a coloring book works great) use Mad Mattr to make the image three-dimensional. Add dots to the butterfly, dirt to a dump truck, or smiles to faces. We've not had Mad Mattr stick to or bleed on paper, but that's no guarantee, so do use caution with what you're sticking it to.

#29. Cockpit
Take about half of your Mad Mattr and spread it out as a cockpit control panel. Use the rest of the Mad Mattr to make buttons, switches, and levers that "operate" your aircraft.

#30. Pretzels
Squish your Mad Mattr into long snakes, then shape each into a pretzel. How big is the largest pretzel you can make? How small is the tiniest?

#31. Paperclips & Googly Eyes
Using any paperclips and googly eyes you have around, make as many creatures as you can this week. Paperclips can double as duck-bills, hair, or mouths–they also make great sculpting tools!

#32. Farm Detective
Collect a handful of animal toys with unique footprints and place them on the table. Squish or roll out most of your Mad Mattr until it is smooth and flat. (Flipping it over will make it perfectly impressionless if you're working on a smooth surface.) Use the rest of the Mad Mattr to make an egg, then break it in half. Have your child cover his eyes while you choose an animal to make tracks around and through the broken egg. Can he detect who accidentally stepped on the egg? Now let him challenge you!

#33. The Shell Game
Have your child use his Mad Mattr to make shells or cups. Let your child watch as you hide a coin or other trinket under one of them. Shuffle them and see if he can correctly guess which shell it is under.

#34. Car Mountain
Use your Mad Mattr to make a mountain for your smallest toy cars. You could use a spoon to smooth out roads and even dig a tunnel through the base of the mountain.

#35. Dog Treats
Use your Mad Mattr to make all kinds of pretend treats for your dog. Standard dog bones could be rolled out and cut with a cookie cutter. Rawhide look-alikes could be twisted together. Small treats could even be sliced off a roll. Not a dog lover? Try making horse treats, giraffe snacks, etc.

#36. Magnetic Rescue at Sea
Make a tiny boat out of paper and tape and fill it with paperclip "people." Use your Mad Mattr to make a tempestuous sea, complete with huge crashing waves. Place your figures to be rescued strategically across the scene, and don't forget to upend the boat or fill it with "water." Next, outfit your lifeboat or rescue helicopter with the strongest magnet you have and rescue all your stranded sailors. (If your magnet is strong enough, don't hesitate to plunge your people completely under the sea for a particularly dramatic rescue.)

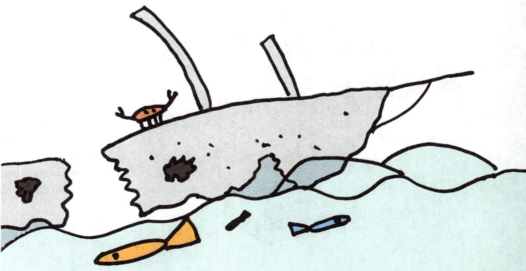

YOUR TOP 4 F.A.Q.S ABOUT NEXT YEAR

THINGS TO THINK THROUGH AS YOU ANTICIPATE THIRD GRADE

So, you're finishing up second grade already? How has it gone for you? Really, we'd love to know! (Plus, you get reward points for your review.) Just jump over to the Second-Grade Curriculum page on our website and scroll down to submit a review.

As you look towards next year, there are a few things that you may want to know.

1. When Can We See the New Kits?

New kits usually release in April. Check our Facebook or give us a call for this year's projection, but it's always in the spring and usually April.

2. Free Customization

If your child has raced ahead in some subjects this year, or if you've realized you need to go back and fill in some gaps, or if you simply don't need more Math-U-See blocks, you'll be thrilled to know that you can customize your kit next year to accommodate that. You'll find full details on our website, but know that it is free and can often be completed online if you prefer to DIY.

3. Do I Need to Take the Summer Off?

Some students finish the grade with an eager passion to jump right into the next grade, and parents contact us asking if that's really okay or if they should take some time off so the child doesn't burn out. We are year-round homeschoolers, so we would definitely be fans of jumping into the next grade here!

However, the truth is that this is a decision only you can make. We can tell you that a long break can quench the thirst for knowledge, so if it were our child, we'd seriously consider moving right into the next grade. However, sometimes a little suspense makes the year begin with a beautiful anticipation!

If you decide to start early, you could consider saving one or two items for your official start date, so that there is still some anticipation.

4. Can I Refill This Kit for My Next Child?

Absolutely! Each year's Additional Student Kit reflects the current year's kit (so the 2019-2020 First-Grade Elite kit and the 2019-2020 Additional Student Kit correlate). If you loved it just the way it was, refill it now before we swap things around for next year. Or, if you prefer, wait for the new kits to launch and then let our team help you figure out what tweaks (if any) need to be made to the standard Additional Student Kit.

We're Here to Help!

If you have other questions for us, would like to share

additional feedback, or you'd like to get in touch for some other reason, don't hesitate to drop us a line or give us a call. (FYI, we also have online chat on our website, if that's easier for you.)

mail@Timberdoodle.com
800-478-0672
360-426-0672

DOODLE DOLLAR REWARD POINTS

WHAT THEY ARE, HOW THEY WORK, AND WHERE TO FIND THEM

If you're one of our Charter School BFFs, we just want to give you a heads up that the following information doesn't really apply to you. Doodle Dollars are earned on individual prepaid orders (credit cards or online payment plans are fine) and don't apply to purchase orders or school district orders. Sorry about that!

Now, with that out of the way, here's the good news. Almost any item you order directly from us earns you reward points! You will earn 1 point for every $1 you spend. 20 points = $1 off a future order!

Some families prefer to use this money as they go, while others save it up for Christmas or for those mid-year purchases that just weren't in the budget.

Can I Earn More Points?
Absolutely! Review your purchases on Timberdoodle.com to earn points. Add pictures for even more points!

We also usually have a few reward point events throughout the year, including the annual Doodle the Catalog contest.

What Can I Spend My Points On?
Anything on our website. These reward points act as a gift certificate to be used on anything you like.

How Do I Get to My Points?
The simplest way is to simply scroll down to the bottom of our website and look for the Doodle Dollars link, listed under Account. If you run into any challenges, please let our team know and we will be thrilled to assist you.

Check our website for the latest information on reward points:
www.Timberdoodle.com/doodledollars

CPSIA information can be obtained
at www.ICGtesting.com
Printed in the USA
BVHW061935090519
547876BV00003B/4/P